THIS ROBOT IS NOT MY FRIEND

The Aversion Bureau: Volume One

S.R. Ringuette

ISBN: 978-0-9879414-1-1

SRR Comics
Second edition

To Danilo!

Thank you so much for your donation! I hope you enjoy the books!

SRR '14

- DEDICATED DEFACEMENT AREA -

Foreword by Aria Bell

At like, three in the morning sometime last month, Sebastien sat up and shouted to an empty room: *"Aria should write the foreword to my book!"*

Ignoring what a stupid thing that is to say, the next day he sent me several frantic messages asking me, Aria, to write a foreword to his book. Actually it was more of a command, and after pausing for a few minutes to compile a list of all the reasons it would be a bad idea, I said yes. Sure I'll throw some words at your book. I agreed, less because I think I'm qualified for such a thing, and more because when Sebastien gets excited about something it's really, really hard to tell him no.

I've never thought myself particularly articulate, but Seb seems to think I am pretty okay and I'd rather not disappoint him. I thought for a good few weeks after I was asked and before I sat down to write this with no idea what to say. This is the first thing most people will see in the Aversion Bureau book and my friend's work is deserving of a good introduction.

I thought I could talk about the little bits of director's insight and commentary Seb's given me during our long conversations, taking place through digital notes passed while at our respective day jobs (he'll tell you all about them if you ask nicely), or I could talk about the superhuman amount of work Sebastien's put into this little strip, and how hard it was to keep up with a break-neck update schedule of almost seven days a week on top of his full time job (he won't). I'm sure he'll get to most that himself though, and I doubt I could sufficiently convey the effect he and his work has had on me and mine here, nor would you want to read such drivel. Well, you would I guess, but you didn't come here to hear it from me.

While I might not be the best at it, one of my favorite things about my friend Sebastien is that now, for the first time in my life, I have someone to talk theory with. Art is the filter I use to process things and it feels more natural for me to talk about comic theory than my own feelings. Considering what you're holding, I assume you'd be more interested in that anyway. Let's do that, then; I will try to be brief.

In my own work I gravitate towards long-form comics for my own reasons, but a majority of the media I consume consists of comic strips, and I am most fascinated by those centered around humor.

A lot of people don't really appreciate comedic works to the extent they should, seeing them as somehow inferior to darker or more serious stories. Comedies, they say, are just vacuous and fleeting, they don't carry the significance of tragedy or drama. Cheap laughs, they don't mean anything.

This is profoundly incorrect.

We find ourselves on a planet defined by its violence, and in a world like this it is very easy to find an audience looking to roll around in misery and self-pity for a while. It's a lot easier to sit in the dark and whine than it is to retain optimism. This is evident in the fact that most people don't think of optimists and pessimists, they list optimists and realists. In storytelling there will always be creators who equate despair with depth. Stories about angst-y protagonists will always sell because it's easier to accept such a character as believable and realistic, since there are so many real life examples. This is a pretty lame state of affairs, I think, and it's a shame our society hasn't evolved enough to see the value of looking on the bright side.

Judging by this, then, works of humor should be considered so much more highly than they are. They're success stories just by virtue of existing. Not only is the writer choosing to turn his experience into something positive for himself, he is creating something that might make another human being laugh or smile, even if it's just for a second. He is creating a little bit more happiness in the world. This is what most cartoonists set out to do. They have enough strength and skill to process their own observations and demons into something positive, then they have enough left over that they try to share that positivity with others who may need it more than they do.

This, I believe, is a most noble endeavor. This is what my friend Sebastien does. I am very proud of him.

Anyway, I've said enough, I'll let you get on with the book. I hope you like it. It's pretty good.

Best,
—Aria Bell
July 2012
Lebanon, TN

Welcome! You are here now, teasing the inner pages of this book with your forthcoming gaze. The dim light of the outside world can penetrate no further and it's nothing but four and eight-panel stalactites for the next 183 pages. I hope I didn't scare you away initially with the back cover of this book. I remember that there was a lot of shouting and ham-fisted sales pitching. I see that it worked.

The excellent foreword you've hopefully just read did all the work I would normally have to do in an introduction and did it wonderfully. Combined with the table of contents across from this page, there isn't much I need to do to prepare you for this book. To that end, let me just tell you that the comic strips in this book were written at a time when I updated *The Aversion Bureau* so frequently that I hardly had time to breathe. I have poured more sweat, tears and *time* upon ***time*** into *The Aversion Bureau* than anything else I've ever worked on. This is because writing and drawing are the only things I never want to stop doing for the rest of my life.

Please enjoy this book, as I'm sure you will, and I hope that some of the joy I get out of creating this little world is imparted onto you as you read about it. Have ***fun.***

This book is dedicated to my endlessly supportive parents
and friends, both online and off, for always giving a damn.
The beautiful bastard who helps me run my website...
and specifically to Frank, for loving Warpgoat the very most of all.

TABLE OF CONTENTS

A DAY AT THE BEACH

"Press Start"

Sir?
Sir can you hear me?
He's up.
H-wha..?
Alright buddy, start talkin'.
We need you to recount everything you can about today, sir.
Oh man.. am I?
Good. I still have my pants.
I don't really know who-
Look at these pictures.
Tell us ***everything...***

"Road Trip"

Ok, let's see...
This morning I was driving up to the lake for a day. Everything was normal.
Hey, this song is *pretty catchy*
♪ Baby baby *baby* ***oooo!*** ♪
♪ *Baby baby ba-*
Oh.
I mean "**In tha hood**". Hood - *uh* - babies.
"Hoes."

"The Arrival"

I parked at the top of a hill overlooking the lake.
Then suddenly...
VromwomwomKRACKwomwo-
!
I wonder if I remembered to bring a frisbee.

"Ominous"

I couldn't remember if I had the frisbee or not so I went to get a closer look at the thing.
WHUMP
It landed.
Whzzzt
Hsss
Pshhh
Then it opened and *sprayed.*
Whzzzt
That's when I knew something was wrong.

"And That's Not All"

Beep.
BOOM
WHY the **HELL** did I *LEAVE THE* ***HOUSE TODAY!?!***

"Hero"

So I hopped the fence and ran down to the beach to see if anybody was ok.
I ran down the hill really fast too. Like a hero would.
Trip
But it was the worst thing I've ever seen.

"Metamorphosis"

I was only trying to help.
IS THERE ANYBODY THAT CAN HEAR ME?
Oh man, oh *man*, where's my *phone?*
Then something started happening to the bodies...
It was like they were being *re-built.*

"The Changed"

They... Came back to life, somehow. But they were *changed.*
Creak
GAH!
There were so many bodies.
Look, please. Just stay away. I know *uh,*
I know *punching-techniques.*
Great ones.

"Blood And Sand"

Slice
AH!
*You **CUT** me!*
They were coming after me.
Stay away!
Whoosh
And they were *everywhere.*
Creeaaak

"Misstep"

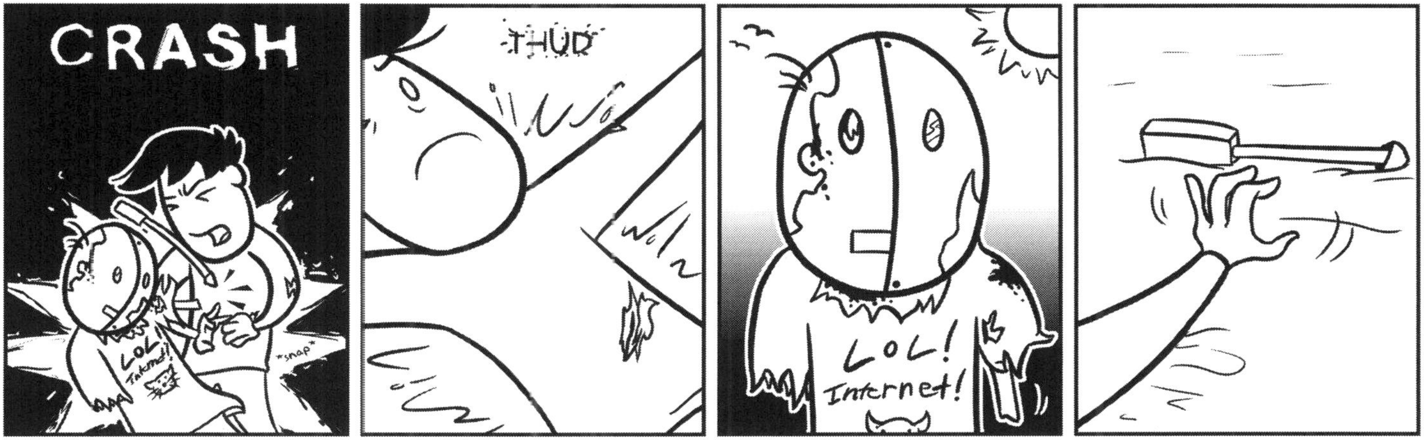
CRASH
LOL! Internet!
snap
THUD
LOL! Internet!

"Beach Justice"

WHACK
LOL Internet
Understandably a little winded, I crawled to the water's edge.
Figured I would be safer there.

"Heads Up"

I had no idea where to go or what to do.
But it's not like I had very much time to think.
Bloop
BANG

"Salvation"

!
And that's where *you* came in.
?
Fuduhduhduh-
Grab my hand bro.

"Lead And Steel"

whhhhhHRRRRR
BRZZZZZZZZZZZZZZT
So.. how ya doin'?
BZZZZZZZZZZZZZZT
Great.
I am, ***very*** confused. Also, a few cuts.
Yeah.
Yup.
Who are you?

"Advanced Technology"

That is not important right now.
Oh hey! Who are *you?*
Oh wow, *cool!* Is that one of those *Men In Black* pens?
Are you going to wipe my memory?
Something like that.
THWACK

"Lucky For You"

Well, that's it. I woke up here. But you know *that* part.
Jerk.
Please, can you tell me what all of that was? *What's going on?*
You may be in luck.
Beep
Standard procedure would be to knock you out again and leave you out back with cab money taped to your forehead.
However...
The director has requested to meet with you.
Was that a *pager?* What year is this?

THE 51st FLOOR

"Follow Me"

This way.
Main Elevator >
< Interrogations
Where are we going again?
I told you. To see the director.
I hope that's a good thing.
- 51 -
We'll see.

"Small Talk"

So what do you *do* here anyway.
Also, where *is* here?
You ask a lot of questions.
Maybe you'd like to discuss the answers over dinner?
Sorry.

"The Director"

DING
Ah! There you are. Please come in.
You are the one we found at the site?
Yes sir.
I've heard that you managed to *kill* one of them, as it were.
Well I hit it in the face.
GOOD *SHOW!*
That is **exactly** the sort of attitude we *need* around here!
The infrequency with which we hit our problems in the face is *undeniable* folly.
Excuse me sir, but your sweater is *adorable*.
?
Noted.

"The Window"

Come to the window my boy.
Do you see it?
See what?
Everything that I have sworn to protect.
The **world.**
Ooh! I see it. The forest?
This is the **Aversion Bureau.** An organization created to protect against *any* and *all* apocalyptic threats.
We save the world.
I am the founder. My name is Thomas Bilge.
Aversion Bureau? Wouldn't ***Apocalypse Bureau*** make more sense?
Oh no, I'm afraid that organization already exists. They *support* the apocalypse.
Oh.
Nice chaps, actually.

"The Digs"

Viewed from the outside this building appears as any other. An office building housing 20 floors of a regular insurance company.
Then there are an additional thirty *windowless* floors before my office on the 51st.
RGI INSURANCE
We operate on *those* floors.
Our headquarters houses an armoury, lab, panic room, gym, interrogations office, barracks, server room, firing range, infirmary, winery, ice cream truck, bean-bag chair room, etc etc.
All of that, yet barely a dozen agents and a skeleton crew of lab technicians and security.
Sometimes I wonder if I went a *tad* over-board on designing the place.
Do the insurance guys ever ask about all the extra floors?
We tell them that those are "Luck Floors".
Luck floors?
It's a Japanese thing.

"The Proposal"

Now tell me your name, good man.
It's Max sir, Max Martin.
Well, I *suppose* that will do. Until I think of something better.
Director Bilge
How would you like to work for me?
W-*what?* **Really?**
I choose to take that as a resounding "yes".
You see, I hand-pick the staff around here and I have a strong feeling that *you* are of the right sort.
Sir, I've never saved the world before. But I will try.
Excellent! Because you know too much.
Try to leave now and I'll have to kick you off of the roof tied to a fridge!

"Welcome Aboard"

Agent Stone will get you set all set up! *Do* enjoy yourself my boy!
We will speak again shortly.
Welcome aboard. Evidently.
Wow. *All of that was crazy!* Was he ***drunk?***
No. You will know when he is drunk. It is an ***ordeal.***
You may find Bilge *eccentric*, as we all do, but he is a dedicated man who truly wants to do good.
You'll learn that in time. I have a map and an access card for you.
Here is your badge. Go home, rest and return tomorrow morning.
This is probably the *coolest thing that has ever happened to me.*

"Forgetting Something"

< Elevator
Hey pretty reception lady, remember this face. It *works* here now!
RGI
SWOOSH
Oh hey! That's my car.
Didn't I leave you at the beach?

"Belonging"

Bro:
Your ride blows. Driving it here sucked. Also, what's with the Bieber CD?
I'm in a club!

"Poker Face"

Almost home. I can't believe that place is just on the outskirts of the city.
What a *convenient* plot device.
Figuratively speaking.
I can't wait to tell my roommate what happened!
...Wait, **damn!** It's supposed to be a *secret* isn't it.
They'll see the cuts!
Jingle
I gotta play this *cool.*
404
Hey, how was the lake?
404
HAHAHA SO *REGULAR!*

"Home Sweet Home"

Oh my God! Max, *why* are you covered in cuts?
Oh *these things?* Some guy tried to take my frisbee.
I fought him.
With my fists!
Ok good night!
SLAM
Max's room.
NO GIRLS Allowed.
Wait, nevermind.
Click
I agreed to let him move in if he pays rent and doesn't hit on me... Maybe I should have added a condition about weirdness.

"En Español"

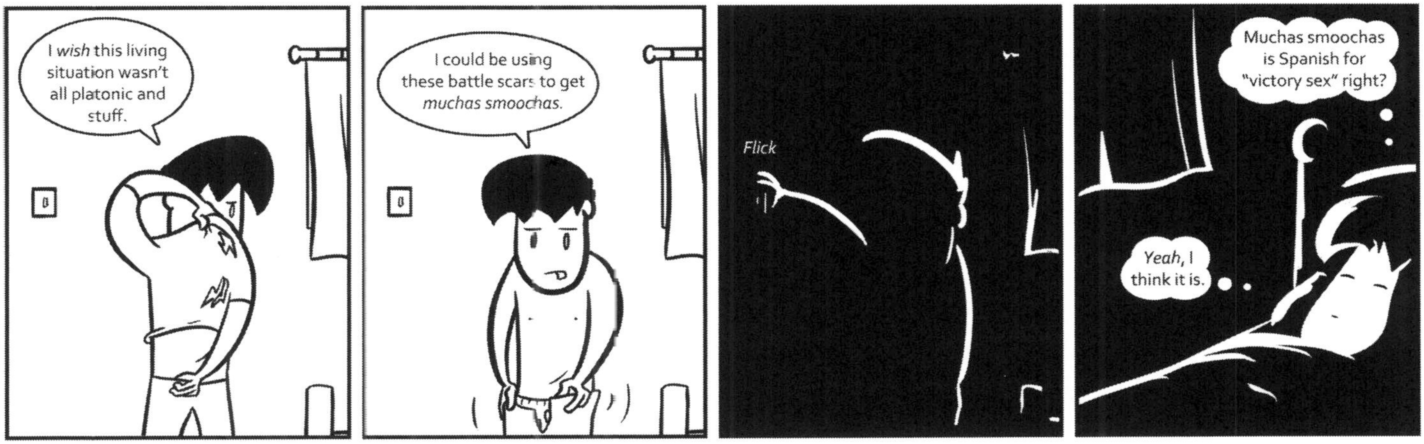
I *wish* this living situation wasn't all platonic and stuff.
I could be using these battle scars to get *muchas smoochas*.
Flick
Muchas smoochas is Spanish for "victory sex" right?
Yeah, I think it is.

Now I Am A Man

A short essay by Max Martin

Now, I am a man.

No longer will I work the full-service gas bar at the behest of those less manly than I. Those middle-managers, they aren't men. They are… *elderly boys*. Yeah, I like that. That's harsh.

Now, I am a man.

No longer will I shop in the *large boys* section when renting formal wear, and when I find hair in the sink, it will be from my **face** or **chest**. Or a lady! *Ooh maybe a lady*…

Now, I am a man.

No longer will I observe the fifteen-minute maximum bounce time at the bouncy castle they set up at the farmer's market on weekends. I'm a God damn ***secret agent*** now and I'll bounce as long as I want to.

Now, I am a man.

When the only girlfriend I've ever had broke up with me in high school for being too sensitive, I vowed to become the ultimate pick-up artist. When that continued to fail me throughout my young adult life I stumbled upon my position at the Aversion Bureau entirely by accident and irrevocably had my confidence boosted.

Sometimes things just work out.

Now, I am a man.

Why, just the other day it was **MY** quick-thinking that saved the day and mine alone. (Such assertiveness is characteristic of men.) I was sent to accompany my co-workers (*co-agents?*) to the home of an elderly Peruvian gentleman who had inadvertently summoned a ***hell-guinea pig*** into his bathroom cabinet during a pan flute solo gone awry. A *hell-guinea pig* being a regular guinea pig that has faced the horrors of the underworld and returned to satiate its blood lust on the flesh of the living.

I'm pretty sure somebody's working on a better name though.

Anyway it was ***my*** ingenuity and quick-thinking that led us to lure the beast into a shallow-drawn bath tub with the aid of some particularly pungent luncheon meats. I found, however, that it is surprisingly difficult to drown anything that isn't an infant, in a bath tub. At this point victory was achieved when agent Davison vigorously (and bravely) suffocated the vicious animal with a nearby plunger.

Sometimes men work in teams, and I am one of those.

A man. Not a team.

There's no 'I' in team.

THE SPADE OF DESTINY

"Dream Time"

*So... **tired**.*
It's dream time.
Ooh! Breasts!
Aah! *Monsters!*
BACON!

"Spade Of Destiny P.1"

pat
pat
SMOOSH

"Spade Of Destiny P.2"

Woah woah **woah!** *What the hell?*
WHACK

"Spade Of Destiny P.3"

Oh my God, I just *destroyed* that thing...
With this *plastic shovel!*
It must be magic.
I must be magic.
Riiiiiiiiiiiiiiiiiiiiip
Oh, **YES.**

"Spade Of Destiny P.4"

SLASH

"Spade Of Destiny P.5"

With this mighty spade I shall construct the sand-castle of *your undoing!*
PSHOOOOOM
You will try.

"Spade Of Destiny P.6"

"Spade Of Destiny P.7"

A NEW MAN

"Dim Realities"

Man that dream *really* turned around at the end...
Now I'm sad.

"Preparation"

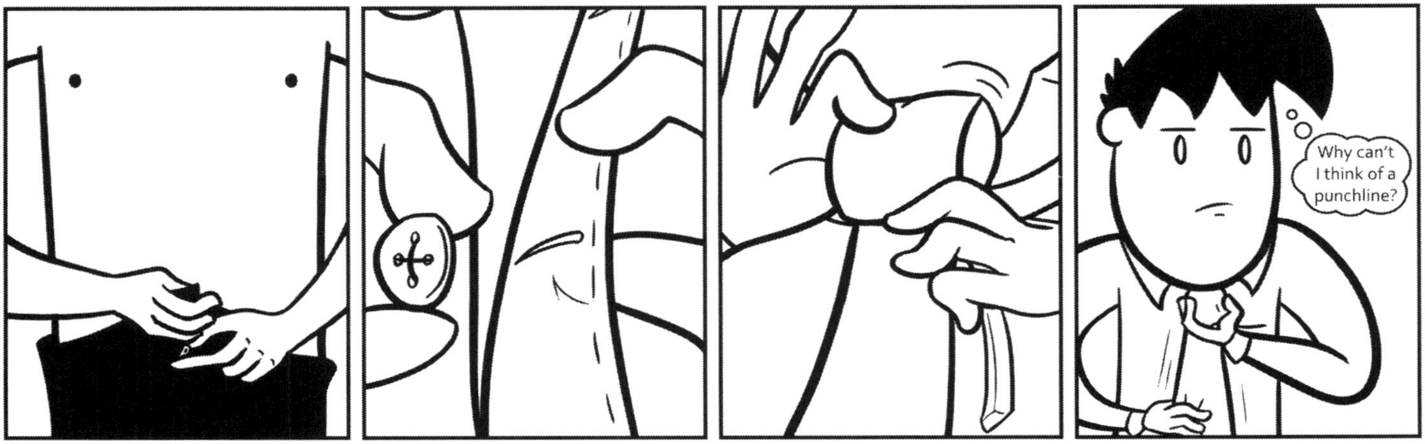
Why can't I think of a punchline?

"Dressed For Success"

Hey, where are you going?
Just work.
You work at a *gas station.*
A cheap one.
What's with the tie?
Oh ye of little faith... I got a promotion!
To super secret agent!
How come? Did you stop playing with yourself at work?
GOODBYE JACKIE.
Because that's *two to three* five minute breaks a day you just can't explain!

"The Plan"

Oh my GOD. I can't believe I forgot about my job.
...My OLD job! I've always wanted to quit that stupid place!
GASSY PUMPS
But I really don't want to be late for my new, awesome job.
So I'll make this quick.

"Free Man"

I'M NAKED!!
I AM A NUDE MAN.
ding ding
CENSORED
I QUIT! I QUIT! GOODBYE FOREVER, JACKASSES!
!
By the wind in my undercarriage, I am a free man!
STILL CENSORED
Hey boss man! Doesn't this bother you?
My genitals flap about in your presence!
4 Aisle
Brian
• Bulk Lotions
• Oriental Cuisine
• Lubricants
4 Aisle
Brian

"Model Employee"

Oh man...
PUM
He's *still* watching.
I can't believe this backfired.
At least I didn't pay for this gas.
There goes my *employee of the month!*
I wonder what he was yelling about.

"5050"

Hey there *pretty reception lady*, I'm here for **work.**
...But I don't know where to go.
Alright.
Well in which department do you work?
The secret one.
Nevermind, I got this. I'll just take the-
Elevators...
BROKEN

"Absent Minds"

Ha ha! What a joke, "broken" I knew that access card had to be for something.
Let's see what's going on... on *floor 31!*
- 31 -
Ding
Man I wish Stone had told me where to meet her. This could take *all day.*
Science sure can be *wacky* can't it?
Indeed!
Hey, *hey guys!* Can you help?
Hey! Where are you going? You left your... ***thingie*** unlocked!

"The Room"

I *really* shouldn't look...
But I will.
!
OH GOD
please help me! *You* ***gotta***
help me! ***THEY WONT LET ME LEAVE.***

"Pure Class"

SLAM
EEP!
Clearly we have a few careless scientists in our midst.
Oh Jesus my heart.
Phew! Usually when beautiful women scare me like that I'm naked. And it's a dream.
I can make one of those things happen right now.

"Reap What You Sow"

Who WAS that guy?
Why is he locked in there?
Although you are technically not authorized to know this, I feel I must explain what appears to be a kidnapping.
If that man ever were to stop drawing, the world as we know it would end.
He knows very well what he got into when he began.
There are more lights in that room... As well as a Gameboy!
He is simply being dramatic.
I am not mentally prepared for this job.
Neither are you physically, follow me to basic training.

"Questions"

Wait! Before we go, *please.*
I *know* that this job is the most completely awesome place I've ever been. But, *the reason I'm even here...*
What happened on that beach? What ***were*** those things? I haven't gotten any answers and I'm having *nightmares.*
Max, I can honestly tell you that you know as much as we do. This is only the third incident we've even been alerted to. But this time, we've acquired samples and our ***top mind*** is working on it as we speak.
I promise that you will have your answers in a few days.

"Fair Warning"

Lastly, you should know that your ham-fisted attempts at flattery have *not* gone by un-noticed.
Really?
Yes.
For every comment you make accumulates to a total in my mind that *only I know*. Then I will show you what seventeen different martial arts can do to a scrotum.
So tread ***lightly.***
I bet *you* tread lightly, because you're so thin. And **hot.**
I'm so sorry I really can't turn it off.

"Enter Dick"

Davison, this is our new recruit: Max.
Sup bro?
Oh God it's you.
My name's **Dick**. Dick Davison, and this...
...Is the arm that once punched *through* a terrorist just to fist bump the hostage on the other side.
Was the terrorist *ok?*
Best make ***SPACE.***
Wait what? *No* dude, he **died**.

BRO

BASIC TRAINING

"Quick Draw"

So...
WHOMP
Lesson one:
Punching *first.*
For the next 48 hours I'll be kickin' your ass bro.
Still... The best... Job -hrkk- **ever.**

"Conditioning"

Lesson two: Guns. *Shooting* guns. Shoot that target.
It's loud the first time.
AAH!
BANG
Did you pee a little?
Yes.
That's normal. Because you missed. We are gonna condition you to pee when you miss.
pat pat

"Practical And Deadly"

Lesson three: Octopus grenades.
Oh *that* sounds awesome! How do I use it?
Just hold on bro.
Whoosh
PAF
Those things can fit in such *tiny* spaces, it's ***crazy!***
It's so sucky and squishy!

"Should Come Naturally"

Lesson four:
Hitting on chicks.
These lessons are starting to get irrelevant.
Hey reception babe, looking **good**. I'm just showing this new guy the ropes. *Sup?*
I'm *very* well, Mr. Davison. Nice to see you again.
So, uh... *hey*. Lookin' for a good time?
whap
I'm the guy from the bathroom wall.

"Meat Sauce"

Lesson five:
Bolognese.
TIME!
sip
ARM WRESTLE
CHEF
You're lucky I don't know what bolognese is...

"Bonding"

Bro, why are you sitting down?
I'm *exhausted.*
Is that *seriously* a Nintendo DS?
Yes. I'm taking a break.
Yo, you got Mario Kart?

ITINNER List
– GUNS ✓
– OCTONADE ✓
– WOMEN ✓
– BOLOGNESE ✓
– BEARING
– RUN-PUNCHING
– WOMEN (x2)
©

CONTAINMENT BREACH

"Stone Cold"

Natalie my dear, take a seat. You look tense.
I've **told** you never to call me that here.
Director Bilge
Do not fret, nobody was around to hear.
I still don't like it.
Where did you leave Maxmillion and that *gormless* beast?
Davison's infamous "Basic Training".
I expect it is too much to hope he has stayed on topic this time.
My dear, that is as likely to happen as this amusing little creature spontaneously **combusting**.
But we are what we are. Always show your best and the best will always come to you.
pat pat
One of those idiots is going to get hurt.
It is likely.

"Don't Shell Me Bro"

That's right. Looks like DK's finally gonna tie down a win.
I dunno Dick. This blue thing just showed up in my inventory. But I think it might be for you.
Booyah! Yoshi pulls it out of his ass again!
No. NO! Not the blue shell! RaaAAHH -
I will literally TEAR YOU IN HALF!
Who the hell is that?
KNOCK KNOCK KNOCK
If it's my adoring fans tell them to come back. The star cup aint even begun.

"No Solicitors"

BANG BANG
Hold the hell on!
Agent Davison! Agent Davison!
There has been a code-green containment breach on this floor!
BANG
You have to ge-AAH AAAAHHHH!
No no no n-
crunch
fwoosh

"Welcome To The Fan"

SLAM
Ok...
Game face.
Listen up, *big hair dude*. I am going to make my way to the weapons lockup on this floor.
Max.
Shut it. You aren't ready for this. Stay here and **don't leave.**
Do *I* get a gun?
Click
I think I want a gun...

"Curiosity"

Some time later...
Ok. I can't stand the waiting any more. I *need* to see what's going on.
Dick may need ***my*** help.
Maybe like 10 minutes, tops.
!
Nope.

"Checking In"

"Great Escape"

"Dead End"

"Black Out"

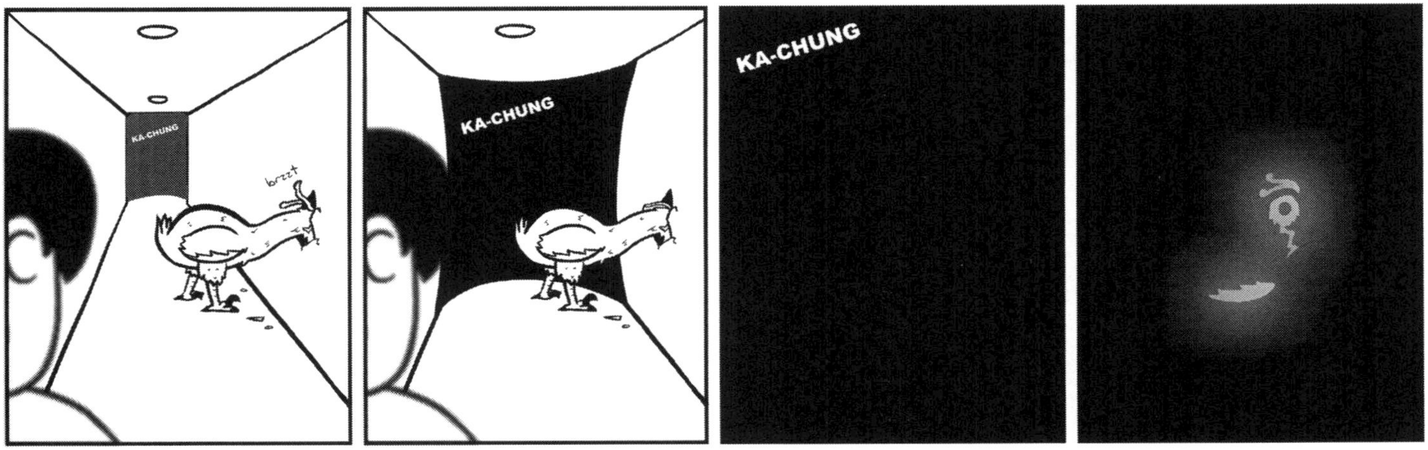
KA-CHUNG
brzzt
KA-CHUNG
KA-CHUNG

"Very Very Frightening"

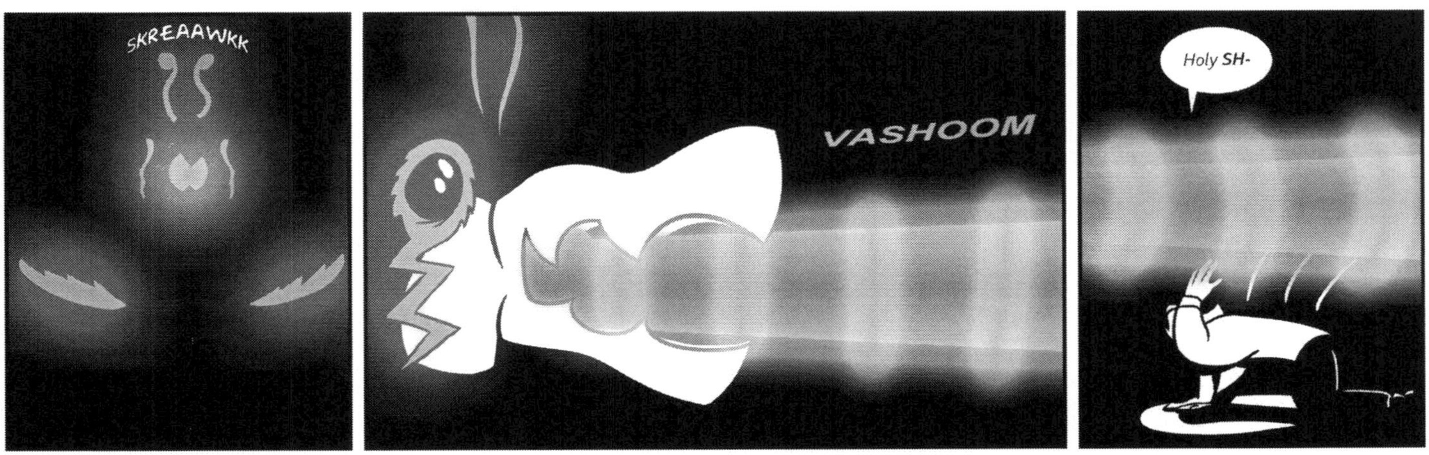
SKREAAWKK
VASHOOM
Holy SH-

"Stealth Bonus"

Skraaawk -
ch-chk
KA-BLAM
Oh thank God! You **saved** me.
What did I tell you to do *dumbass?* **Stay put.**
But I couldn't leave you alone out here!
You ***are not*** ready for this, bro.
click
Ooh! A flashlight!
Let's tell ghost stories.
How are you alive?

"Direct Hit"

Look, I'm *impressed* that you aren't dead yet. You must be doing *something* right.
But we have to get the *hell* off this floor, got it?
I'm sorry, I make stupid jokes when I'm nervous, and right now I'm about ready to throw up all over you.
Yeah it's ok, let's go.
I have this *constant* desire to be a hero but I just don't have any skills to back it up!
Yeah, ***whatever***, we can teach you those. Just hurry up 'cause that wasn't the only o-
Oof!
SHOOM

"Back Up"

Dick! **Get up!** God **dammit!**
I'm sorry.
This is where I die.
I have at least a dozen regrets.
Skrawwk!

"Fishin'"

BreAAwk?
SWITCH
clack
KRACK
Excellent timing, looks like the team upstairs got the lights working again.
Thank you! ***Thank you!*** *Thank you!*
You have *five seconds* to cease this embrace.
Five...
I think I love you.

"Denoulusion"

Davison has been taken to the infirmary, he is in stable condition.
Tough as he is bothersome.
As for those creatures...
Director Bilge
Liquidated assets of the mad geneticist "*Doctor Birdimals*" whose operations we foiled a year ago. Bilge didn't want to put them down.
It felt too *genocidey*.
Either way that was the only breeding pair and clearly they've been dealt with.
I will be conducting a thorough review of containment protocols. You are free to go home, consider your basic training *complete*.
Yes, ***do*** get a good night's rest Maxworth. Try not to think of birds.
Or **electricity**.

!
?

DAVISON'S DIARY

(top secret bro)

June 3

- Somebody brought their dog to work today.
  It was awesome. (Benched 350 today!)

June 20

- I met a British lady today. I've never met one before.
  I thought all British people looked like Bilge.

~~March~~ August 8

- Dear diary. Hey what's up? Hah.

August 30

- (Lyrics) AND so I re-gret, that in the times that we met,
  ~~I never showed~~ you - ~~showed you~~... (G, C, F, A)
  AND I regret you'll never know, about the feelings that I hold-
  - and what a strong man can keep, in his heart.

Sept 1

— Dear diary sometimes I'm sad.

Sept 9

— I think the new guy Max, is starting to like me. Not like I care. But 's cool. He's a bro.
Also- Dear diary agent Stone was a total babe today, She scares me. It's hot.

Oct 22

— I left my songbook out and Max found it. He was starting to laugh so I broke a chair over his head.

Friendship setback! :(

THE GREATEST ACCOUNTANT WHO EVER LIVED

"Regrets"

10:00 pm
08:00 am
Nobody ever died when I worked at the stupid gas station.
06:00 pm
02:00 am
Ok, well nobody ever got ***eaten***.

"Good Morning"

Sigh... gotta get up sometime I suppose...
Skreeawwk!
SWEET AND SOUR JESUS NO!!!
Max!? What are you yelling about?
There's a **bird** in my window!
So?
Please come in here and ***kill it with a tissue.***

"Wake Up Call"

Bzzzt
BZZT
Hello Mr. Martin, you missed work yesterday.
Oh, has it been a day *already?* I'm sorry I...
Stil under the bed sheets?
I AM NOT!
Whoosh
Listen, I understand. This is a predictable reaction when confronted with something a civilian may never see in their life. It has happened to the best of us. Report in right now and I'll show you something that may just help you ease back into things.
Wow, Stone, I've never seen you *care* like this before. **Thanks**. It means alot-
I'm reading from a script.
Oh. Well ok. Yeah I'll come in then.
Bye.

"Setting Things Straight"

Welcome back, Mr. Martin.
Hey.
Now, as you are *aware*, our bureau is built on top of an insurance company, its name: Really Good Insurance ®
Really good *insurance!?*
Seriously, it's great.™
This is a *real* company, entirely autonomous in operation but still *owned* by Bilge. In fact the bureau is funded jointly by the profits of RGI **and** Bilge's own personal wealth.
Oh... Is that enough?
Just enough, and we budget accordingly.
Due to the secretive nature of our operations upstairs, we are all assigned auxiliary positions within RGI as cover. I '*work*' in human resources, agent Davison '*works*' in sales and we've put *you* into accounting.
I don't even really know what accounting *is*.
And Dick Davison couldn't sell a parachute to a rich man falling from the ***sky***.

"Package Deal"

Now keep in mind that you need never actually come to the insurance building with the intention of working. It is just what you can tell civilians when they ask what you "do for a living".
That *really* sounds like my kind of job.
I am going to show you to your office now. You can spend the day here and get acquainted.
Really? My own office?
-Hi, I'm Jim, the intern.
I'm sorry, I thought this office was empty. I've been keeping things here.
...Can I get you a coffee, sir?
Wow! This guy's *great!* Does he come with the room?
Sure why not.

"Pop Quiz"

So Jim.
Yes, sir?
What *is*... accounting?
Well, *basically* it's the process of recording and reporting financial information about a business to its shareholders and managers.
...But don't you *know* that? I mean, you work here. This is *your* office.
Hah a ***right!*** Just testing you.
Hey Jim.
Sir?
In your time here has anyone ever put an *octopus* on your face or told you to hide from giant, *electric* ***murderbirds?***
No sir. In fact I don't think **anybody** will
Then I will become *the **greatest accountant** who ever lived.*

"Overtime"

My loyal assistant left for the night, but I remained. For I intended to become the ***greatest*** accountant.
So valuable to the company that the bureau could never ask me to return to the scary job upstairs.
I brought pencil to paper with furious purpose.
I broke the spines of *countless* record books and drank deep in their knowledge like so many old souls.
But I came to a terrible realization...
It's all just a bunch of **dumb** books with ***BULLSHIT*** *numbers in them!!*

"Cracking The Code"

3:00 am
Z Z z
Buh.. Bwah? Where *am* I?
Wait - wait a minute... I think I **get** it now.
It really ***is*** bullshit. ***Nobody*** understands it!
Everyone's just *bullshitting* each other! **Nobody** understands how accounting works - they're just a bunch of ***bullshitters!***
That makes so much sense!

"Transformation"

I had torn down the veil.
I knew their secrets.
To become the ***greatest accountant who ever lived***...
I would have to put on the biggest show.
On my shoulders rest the hopes of me.
I'm gonna account my ***ass*** off.

"Clarification"

Good morning sir! -
Uh.. What is this?
What did you do?
!
WHAT IS THIS?
Calculo Dominum
THIS IS ACCOUNTING!!
KICK!
- On the other hand, what do I know? I'm just the intern.

"And I Shall Name Him Leonardus"

Jim! The lord of accounting demands sustenance!
Bring me a coffee and a live baby seal!
Um... Yes sir! Right away sir.
Bang!
An impressively short amount of time later...
Very good, now leave us be.
shoo
sip
so CUUUUTE!
HUG

"Compromise"

Damn it, Jensen! I said I wanted those *damn* numbers on my ***damn*** desk by ***DAMN*** O'CLOCK!
I will now assert my dominance with a physical act!
Calculo Dominum
Calculo Dominum
Well *this* isn't happening.
phew
Calculo Dominum
OFFICE DAYCAR
FLIP

"Phoning It In"

Mr. Martin, others in the department have been voicing *concerns* about the report you sent out this morning.
Concerns? This thing is *covered* in numbers.
But they don't seem to ***mean*** anything.
That's absurd! I was advised by ***TOP MEN***. That's it, I'll call them right now! You'll see!
Sir, that is a *child's* ***pretend-telephone***. Where did you even get that?
Quiet, they're connecting me.
Two plus two equals four!
Yes, YES that's exactly what I've been trying to tell them. It's ***all over*** the report!
The cow says: Mooo!
Alright now you're getting off-topic. I'll call you back.
My associate is **super** dissapointed in you Jim.
Did you *hear* the cow?
Yes sir.
Darn ***right*** you heard him.
click

"Whatever Happened To"

That's it, bro. Game over. You're done.
Who are *you* to talk to me like that?
I am **KING here!**
Look, you're coming ***back*** upstairs to your ***real*** job and I don't ***care*** if you're scared.
This is what you ***do*** now.
Dick!? Thank ***GOD*** you're alive! But, you don't *understand* I -
No! ***NOOO!*** You can't do this! I am **drunk** on ***power***!
..And that ***whiskey*** I found in the ***desk***.
LIFT

"To Be Continued"

Dark whispers fill my thoughts.
Where do they come from?
I think I know.
Calculo Dominum
Do I dare take up the mantle of a mad god?
I am Jim the intern no longer.
Today I am reborn.

THE HALLOWEEN PARTY

"The Halloween Party Part 1"

This story begins on the night whimsy wins, in the battle with work-a-day drear.
'Tis Halloween night and the office alights with a party of holiday cheer.
Although hard as he tried, young Max was denied, his window to average man's work.
FBI
Fox M.
There's no day in the year that he'll have more fun here, when booze and the costumed collide.
And of course there are those who stick up their nose, at the prospect of partying fun.
But that's nothing compared to a friend's ill-prepared, speech spun on how they'd have a ton.
So good times prevailed, stubbornness failed-
And party games ruled the day.

"The Halloween Party Part 2"

There's something to know, about old Thomas Bilge. Adult beverage should not touch his lips.
Usually under-control, by Natalie Stone but tonight her watch was remiss.
At a party like this, a thing you surely won't miss, is alcohol in droves and in spades.
And when self con-trol fails its saving-roll, in a river of liquor Bilge wades.
A sip of the stuff is more than enough,
glug glug
to make beast from what's otherwise man.

"The Halloween Party Part 3"

An alternate ego now stood in his place, begotten of whiskey, it was wearing his face.
This persona is not completely unknown, and familiar to those who've had Bilge in their home.
Like Jekyll to Hyde or sharp-stick to gun, old Thomas Bilge was now *'Binge Drink-ing-ton'*.
An exceptional gentleman, of the right-proper sort, but to in-sult his honour may cut your life short.
And that was exactly what Dick Davison did. Laughing hysterically at what he thought were ***costume*** monocle and lid.

"The Halloween Party Part 4"

Binge's anger exploded, unbridled, unabated. Mockery was something that was just not tolerated.
Dick didn't even move, put in shock by it all...
HEAVE
Then Binge shifted his weight,
HO
and put him straight through the wall.

"The Halloween Party Part 5"

With not a moment to spare to quell old, shirtless fury, Max got to their only hope in a hurry.
!
She knew what to do, she had seen this before, she had to act fast before more friends hit the floor.
And there was only one way to make the man again tame, distract him until sobriety came.
"***Tell us a story!***" Was her commanding request, Binge stopped abruptly, at her behest.
For this was the one thing, he could not resist. When it comes to good stories, old Binge has a list.
What a splendid idea, you have there my dear!
But there are so many, which would ***you*** like to hear?

WHERE IT ALL BEGAN: PART 1

"The Big Distraction"

Hmm.. We're going to need something long, long enough to get it all out of his system.
Tell u
Tell us how you **FOUNDED** THE ***BUREAU!***
Oh heavens that **IS** a long one isn't it? Well let us all find a seat and get ready, shall we?
One sec, I gotta scrape up Davison.
Do what you must, we'll meet up in the *bean-bag chair room!*
CLAP
Max, is that.. *You*? I musta drank a ton 'cuz I just had a *crazy* dream that the boss took off his **shirt** and threw me through a ***wall***.
No kidding? Well the *whole* room just had the same dream.
Woah, *really?* That's like... ***Inception***.

"Oh Yeah Those Guys"

We have a bean-bag chair room?
Who *was* that big angry old guy?
I *think* he owns the company. Don't see him much though.
sip
nod nod
Man, I hope we're union.

"He Wasn't Joking"

Ok big guy, just in here.
Oh man, is it story time? I ***love*** story time.
Bean-bag chair room
Holy- I didn't *really* believe it until now.
Yeah bro it's a *comfy* son of a bitch in there.
You're just in time! Pull up a bag!
I have a strong feeling that this has happened before.
Bro, why do you think he ***built*** this room?

"Unnecessary Detail"

Yo this aint so bad, once I spent **four days** in here learning the origins of *mustache grooming*.
That's *brutal!*
No *way*, you're still gettin' paid and he won't notice if you fall asleep.
Best four-day nap ***ever***.
Alright, so, *The Founding of The Aversion Bureau* eh? Let us start at the ***very*** beginning.
I remember the womb as being... ***Humid***.
WOAH!! *Too far back!*
Just be thankful that he skipped the conception this time.

"The Tale Begins"

Alright well, we'll skip forward in the story although I **assure** you that the conception is quite a *riveting* yarn.
It was a very long time ago, back when everybody's memories were in sepia tone.
I was born into an ***extremely*** wealthy family, I needed never to work a day in my life.
But that is not to say that I didn't.
By eight years old my first mustache was really beginning to fill out.
Patriotic aspirations to fight for Queen and Country began to boil in my veins.
And as luck would have it, I was given the chance to follow this calling.
At fifteen years old I was the youngest soldier in my platoon to tea-bag Hitler's corpse.

"The Good Ol' Days"

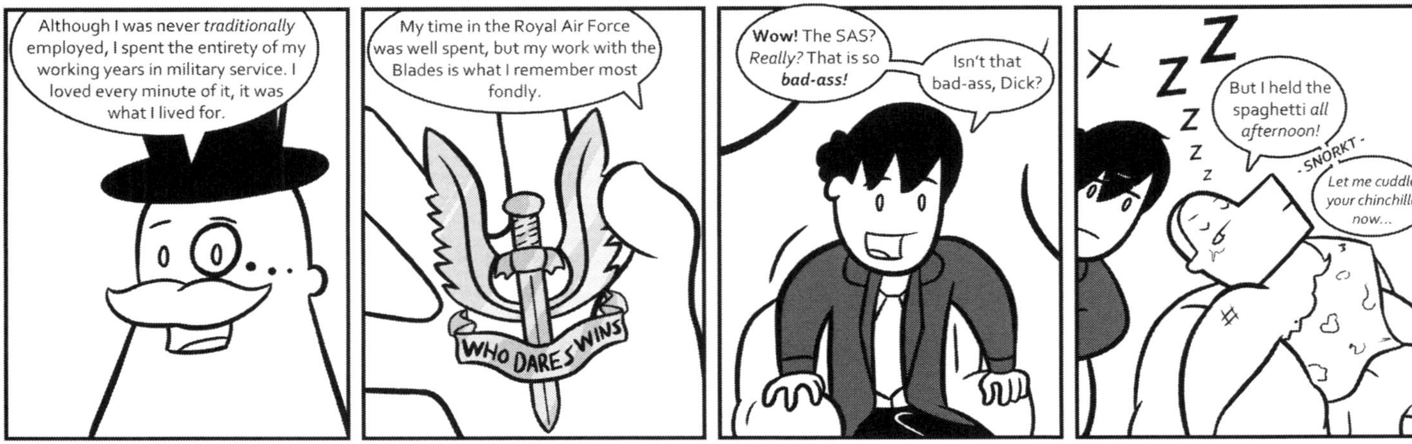

Although I was never *traditionally* employed, I spent the entirety of my working years in military service. I loved every minute of it, it was what I lived for.
My time in the Royal Air Force was well spent, but my work with the Blades is what I remember most fondly.
WHO DARES WINS
Wow! The SAS? *Really?* That is so ***bad-ass!***
Isn't that bad-ass, Dick?
Z Z Z Z Z
But I held the spaghetti *all afternoon!*
- SNORKT -
Let me cuddle your chinchilla now...

"Killing Time"

When I eventually reached retirement age I fought to keep my job, but they eventually convinced me that my continued service *"just wasn't fair"* to the bad guys.
Alas, time makes bitches of us all.
I tried to remain active into my retirement, I kept in touch with old army mates as a strategic advisor and friend.
But mostly I whittled away the years at a prominent gentlemen's club.
We smoked cigars, drank fine drinks...
And did as bored gentlemen with lots of money do.
SMACK
We dueled ***incessantly***.

"The Challenger"

By sword or gun, animal hands or our own fists,
we dueled for honour, money and oftentimes *even more.*
I'll have you know I was at the top of the ladder! *So to speak.*
I was undefeated.
But that reputation did not stop an over-confident international businessman from stumbling *drunkenly* through the doors one fateful night.
He wagered a *hefty* prize of personal property on my defeat.
I planted him into the earth in hopes that yet more fools would grow from his roots and come to challenge me.

"Across The Pond"

As it turned out, the property that my challenger had wagered was *this* very company! RGI insurance and *all* the land it was built upon.
WALL OF WINNINGS
But this was just another win in a long, inebriated streak of victory, so I did not give much thought to what I had *really* won that night.
It wasn't until two years later that I ever even *saw* the place. A decade of drinking, *combat* and ***drunken combat*** had made me so weary. I was depressed and found myself quite stuck in a rut.
glug
glug
So I hopped on a plane to North America to have a look at the largest prize I had ever won from a gentleman's duel. I hoped it might end up being **exciting**. Might give me a reason to wake up in the morning...
Now, *pay attention* because this is where the story gets REALLY interesting.
Allllright. I think that's just about enough story time for one night. It's time you two got home. Binge is sober enough now; with some rest he'll be fine.
But! I want to hear
Wake up Davison and get out.

"Inglorious Exit"

Thank you my dear, I was getting *quite* drowsy, will you make me hot cocoa?
Yes.
Also my nipples are cold.
We'll get you a sweater.
Man that story was *so awesome*, and I can't **believe** Bilge was in the **SAS**! They're the UK's most famous special forces unit! **SO**. ***COOL***.
Only.. Now I'm not sure if I should feel safer here or be worried I'll get *thrown through a wall*.
Yaaawn. Don't worry bro, this is the *only* time "***Binge***" has ever attacked one of us. It was my fault for laughing at him. Stone keeps such a tight leash on it, ya know?
I thought he was just jokin' for Halloween.
You know what's funny though, I heard this story before. Stone stopped it at the *exact* same spot.
That's not very funny.
What? Did you want a **punchline?**
Well, yeah.
To be continued...

A MEETING OF THE MIND

"The Best Part Of Waking Up"

How's the hangover?
Like a dozen monkeys playing crappy slap-bass in my skull.
Director Bilge
I'll get you a coffee.
Thank you.
sigh
Director Bilge
You know I've always found coffee to be an **excellent** *booze-flavourer*.
No.
Director Bilge

"Vestilagiubba"

Today I feel *whimsical!* I will find another to share in my whimsy!
Maxwell, do ***you*** feel whimsical today? Does my whimsy wash over you?
I NEED AN ADULT!
I propose that we exchange scandalous tales concerning former and current colleagues whos names have fallen into disrepute.
You... You mean *gossip?* Ok...
Alright, here goes: Once I walked into agent Davison's office and found him singing the clown's aria from *Pagliacci* to himself in the mirror whilst crying.
Your breath smells like coffee and bourbon.

"Let The Bars Fall Where They May"

Hey there reception lady. Wow you've sure got a ***great*** view of the vending machine from there, betcha seen a **lot** of transactions.
You know, you can tell a lot about a man from his choice in candy bar.
BANG
- THWUMP -
Oh, a ***Butterfinger***. Well, it's suggestive... But kinda in a gross way.
STUFF
Look, I'm sorry, I was hoping for a **Mr. Big**..
Or like, a *Hugepeniscommitment* bar.

"Serpentine Preserves"

HNNNNGH!
Max, I *can't* open this can of snakes! I think it's stuck, help me out!
heh heh...
Can.. Can of *snakes*? Like those prank, spring-loaded snakes?
-snk- Yeah bro!
Ok sure. *I guess.*
NNNNNNNGH
tee-hee!
- pop -
What the- This can's full of *JAM!*
HAHA! *Bet you were expecting* ***snakes****, weren't ya?*
I think you got this backwards.

"Off We Go"

Hey I just got a message from Stone, looks like it's time for that meeting with the research department and that "top mind" she mentioned.
bap
Oh, looks like you finally get to find out what happened to you back on that beach.
Bro.
You know, I had almost forgotten about that, aside from the nightmares.
But without it, I wouldn't even be here.
So I can live with a bladder-voiding fear of beaches.
Weird. *Really* weird.
So what's this guy like? The "***top mind***" ?
But *you're* weird, ***agent Stone*** is weird and **Bilge** is a psychiatrist's Magnum opus. *How bad could he be?*
Weird? Don't kid yourself bro, I'm ***awesome***.

"Gobsmacked"

ROOM W
Ok, well **this** is the conference room. But Stone should already be here.
Maybe she's just-
SON OF A B-
Typical.

"Weak Point"

This is **so** like you *ladybro*, you give ***us*** the ice queen ball-buster treatment but whenever *Andersen's* involved you ***tart*** it up like you're sixteen and he's a quarterback!
I'm sure that I have *no idea* what you are referring to, Davison.
But if you value your capacity to produce viable sperm I would just drop it.
- creak -
Welcome.
Uh, *hey*.
Yeah. Sup, bro?
Hiiiiii Wade.

"That Explains A Lot"

Commencing presentation.
-click-
Scoria
POP culture
Subject: The Scoria.
Human corpses reconstructed and re-animated by nano-technology.
Victims are "infected" with nano-bots prior to death.
Upon death corpse is crudely reconstructed from self-contained materials and metals found in the body.
The technology remains dormant until subject death to avoid expendature of limited energy reserves combating immune system.
Completion and quality of reconstruction vary dependant on concentration of nano-bots and state of deceased human host.

"Projectors In The Dark"

Method of distribution previously unknown.
3
2
1
Primary and secondary sites of incident yielded no evidence.
Only visual account of tertiary incident indicates delivery of nanites via air-borne aerosol dispenser combination explosive.
After distributing payload delivery system detonates, killing victims, beginning process.
BOOM
Origin of design: Unknown.
Method of command: Unknown.
Purpose: Unknown.

"Cliff Hanger"

The Scoria appear entirely mechanical with no digital components or communication devices.
Initial power source somehow intrinsic. Extended operational viability unclear.
Understanding of mobility and animus incomplete.
Crudeness of design and relative small scale of incidents suggest technology is being experimented.
POP culture
Brashness of trials suggest limited window of time before technology makes noticeable leap forward.
-click-
One final order of business.
!
Agent Max Martin is infected with Scoria nanites.

DOCTOR DOCTOR

"Under My Skin"

!!!
Holy JESUS! Are you serious!?
Are they inside me right now?!?
swat
Wow... That's...
That's a lot to take in...
You're brilliant, Wade.
clasp
SHUT UP! Can we please focus on me right now? I'm infested with nano-whatsits!
I'm gonna die and turn into a robot zombie.
What the hell is wrong with you?

"Just To Be Sure"

Oh man this is *too much*. Are you **absolutely** sure? You said that the bomb blows up and kills the infected people to turn them!
But I wasn't anywhere ***near*** the bomb! Maybe those nano things didn't reach me either!
We act on the assumption that you are infected.
Come to my lab for testing.
Insufficient data.
Oh... Yeah ok let's go.
Good luck bro, and don't get the rubber glove test.
You don't want that one.

"Lesson Learned"

I don't ***get*** why you dress up like this for Wade, he doesn't even *notice* you.
*He doesn't notice **anybody**.*
At least when ***I*** first got here I was mackin' on you for like a *week straight*.
Until I broke your chin.
Yeah...
It never did look quite right after that...

"Prepare Your Veins"

This is your lab?
We're here. Take a seat. Blood test.
A portion of it, yes.
Wow... That's uh.. That's *quite* a selection of needles.
Some of those are pretty.. **Big**. What are they all for?
Ambience.

"The Greener Grasses"

I can't believe this, another ***ridiculous*** situation I get dragged into. I wish I was never even brought to this **stupid** bureau...
Had you not been rescued you would be dead. Or Scoria.
Yeah but I've been here for like a *week* and I've almost died ***three times***.
Then your life was better before.
Well, not *exactly*. I never got around to post-secondary and I worked at a gas station for minimum wage.. My only hobby was video games...
*And I masturbated a **lot**.*
You are thankful for more than you know.

"Science"

Hey Wade what's up?
Scaninnating.
Results pending.
SCANINNATOR
That's *uh*... That's not the same thing as the problem I came to you with last month is it?
A prostate exam.
To check for microscopic robots.
Yeah that one.
Yup.
Yes it is exactly the same thing.

"Getgetgetgetgetchudrunk"

What you gon' do with all that junk? All that junk inside yo-
Hah! Is that *seriously* your ring tone?
flip
Shut up, this is Bilge's phone.
Hello?
-yes.
Did you hail it?
Damn it, we'll be right there.
Davison we're needed on the roof, an unidentified aircraft is flying a bit too close to ignore.
!
Ooh! *I hope it's aliens!*

AversionBureau.com

"I Delete Those Right Away"

Well that was *quite* a scan.
I feel very... *Scannish.*
Hey that *thing*, it looks **through** me and stuff right?
It didn't take any *regular* pictures did it? Like when I was ***sans-towel***?
No.
Are you just saying that to make me feel better?
Yes.
Wow! I think we're going to get along ***great***!

"Perspective"

I still cannot identify it.
Whatever it is, it isn't responding to our communications. We should assume that it is hostile.
OH MY GOD BRO IT'S COMING RIGHT FOR US!!
Wait, have I got these 'round the right way?
Ok yeah.
It's coming right for us.

"For Scientific Purposes"

Do you have the results yet?
Patience.
Sorry, I'm just anxious.
I could offer you a comforting plush animal.
Oh wow, actually I'd ***really*** li-
KA-BOOM
Except that there's only one and it's mine.

"First Strike"

VA-SHOOM
RGI
KA-BANG
KER-HEAVE

"Off My Chest"

Agent Martin. You have the Scoria nanites in your body.
Though in much lower concentration than the subject found nearer to the blast radius.
Extreme caution is still advised.
I will begin working on a cure immediately. I expect success.
Thanks... No really, ***thank you***.
I owe you people my ***life***. I'm sorry, I have *no reason* to complain about being here.
I've been nothing but ungrateful.
Alright.
Yeah.
*Ok, so... **yeah**.*
Cough - **I wonder what's going on up on the roof?*

"Pays To Prepare"

I'm out!
Ka-Chink
VROOOSSHHHHHH
..Though it appears that our assailant is retreating...
GET BACK HERE SHADOWY-MYSTERIOUS-*FLYING*BRO!
*Imma punch you **so** hard-*
***Uh**, so hard!*
That-
***Damn,** I really should write these down before-hand.*

"Deliberation"

Ok *that* thing *had* to be with the Scoria! It just adds up, bros!
Hold on.
We have no idea *what* that was. We cannot just assume it was related to recent events. Coincidence or not.
It is also *exceptionally* unlikely that they would know where to find us.
Additionally the aircraft was only detected by line of sight.
Invisible to our scanners.
Troublesome.
There musta been someone else at that beach!
They *know* Max survived and they *know* we saved him!

"Deliberation Part 2"

...And *as for* agent Martin?
Presence of Scoria technology confirmed.
Currently developing treatment.
Excellent.
As for the rest of us, we *prepare*. What we saw today was not an attack, but reconnaissance. Testing our defenses.
If it *were* an agent of the Scoria it was either here tying up loose ends or punishing our interest in their activities. It will return in force.
So we're *sittin' ducks*, huh? We don't know **where** they come from or **when** they're gonna try to stop us...
But when they *do*, I gotta whole-sale barrel a-whoopass **RIGHT HERE.**

"Do You Think Anyone Will Notice"

RGI Insurance parking lot.
The next day.
What-
What the?
Bill!
Hey, Bill!
Are you SEEING this?
Yeh Bob?
There's a smoking crater in the roof of the building!
Ah.. Yeah I see whatya mean.
Well what the hell happened?
Best not to ask questions.
Learned that the day I found a giant bird's skeleton in the dumpster.

Andersen's Log_

<Entry\I43>

Research on Scoria technology progressing quickly. Technological understanding precipitating. Motives remain clouded. Technology crude yet effective. Signature of origin absent though currently irrelevant. Every aspect of Scoria presentation, arrival, activities devoid of clear purpose. Frustrating.

<Entry\M11>

Attended black tie event in 35th floor lunch room. Observed coworkers consuming mechanically separated pork rolled in light pastry. Supposedly tasteful.

Results inconclusive following 30 trials.

<Entry\I48>

Sheer volume of communications received from agent Stone irrelevant to bureau-operations necessitates storage on external hard drive. Retained for posterity.

<Entry\S21>

Agent Davison makes repeated attempts to store muddy sporting equipment in lab.

Wall-mounted sentry turrets now set to fire warning shots.

<Entry\S45>

Attempted psychological profiling of assumed Scoria mastermind proves inconclusive time sink. Focus shifted to cure symptoms over cause.

<Entry\Y14>

Agent Davison admitted to infirmary citing listening problems.

<Entry\O09>

Commencement of construction on Scoria cure.
Multitude of scientific assumptions made. Uncomfortable.
Computational cycles from main processing cluster devoted
to digitally genuflect indefinitely.

Humour. Machines have no god.

<Entry\U25>

A great clock is ticking.
Its hands our shadows.
Its face our sun.
I will save my friends.

A
DICK DAVISON
CHRISTMAS

"Scrolling Text"

THE AVERSION BUREAU
PRESENTS
A SOON-TO-BE
HOLIDAY CLASSIC
DICK DAVISON
RUINS
CHRISTMAS
...AND THEN
SAVES
IT
Christmas Eve
MANPORIUM
OPEN

"Goodness In Every Barrel"

"Legally Bro"

"That Distinctive Sound"

SHUT!
? ? ?
NO! Not my stringy cheese!
!

"It's On"

Damn it mousebro! What are you doin'?
Bring back my FOOD!
! ! !
WHAM
Of course you realize, this means war.

“Time Related Pun”

-tok
Ahah! Gotcha!
tick-
-tock
tik-
GRAB
SMASH

“Wily”

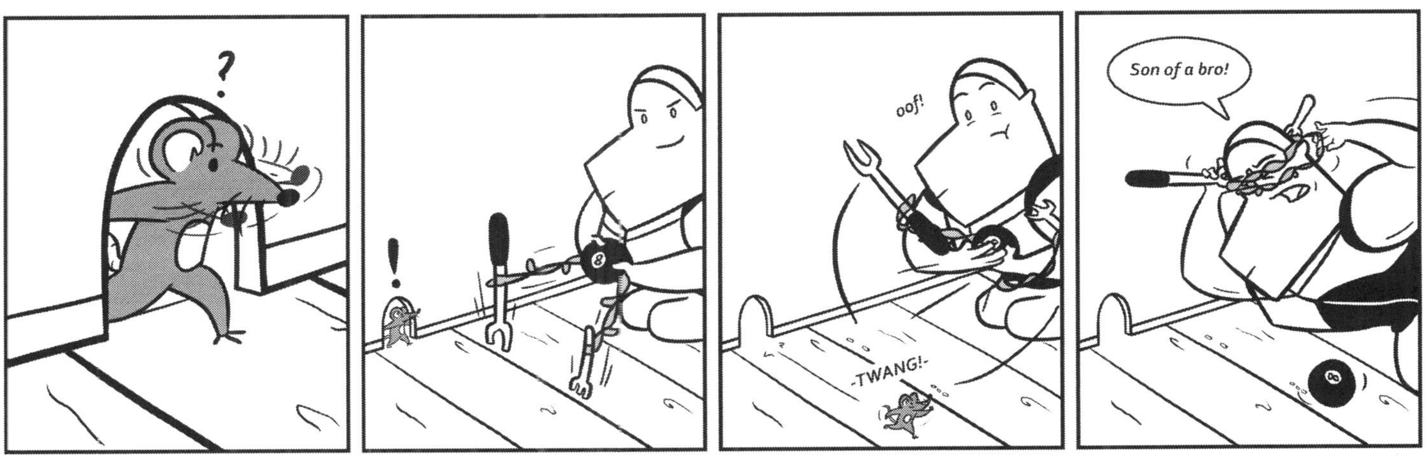
?
!
oof!
-TWANG!-
Son of a bro!

"The Direct Route"

AAAUGH I am SO done with you!
CRASH
You and me man, right now! Mano-a-mouseo! I... Oh.. Oh no.
You were only stealing from me.. To have Christmas dinner with your lady!
Don't worry, little mousebro. I will make this right.
snif

"A Nondenominational Miracle"

-shoompfh-
*BUMP
Merry Christmas mousebro!
...And er, lady mousebro.

"Very Merry Indeed"

This is the best Christmas *ever*.
I wonder what the others are up to...
Oh Rick, of **COURSE** I'll marry you!!
Jackie you make me the happiest man in the world!
No, you *jackasses*! Shoot the **medic** first!
-Happy New Year! SRR

CLUBBIN'

"Not As Cool As It Sounds"

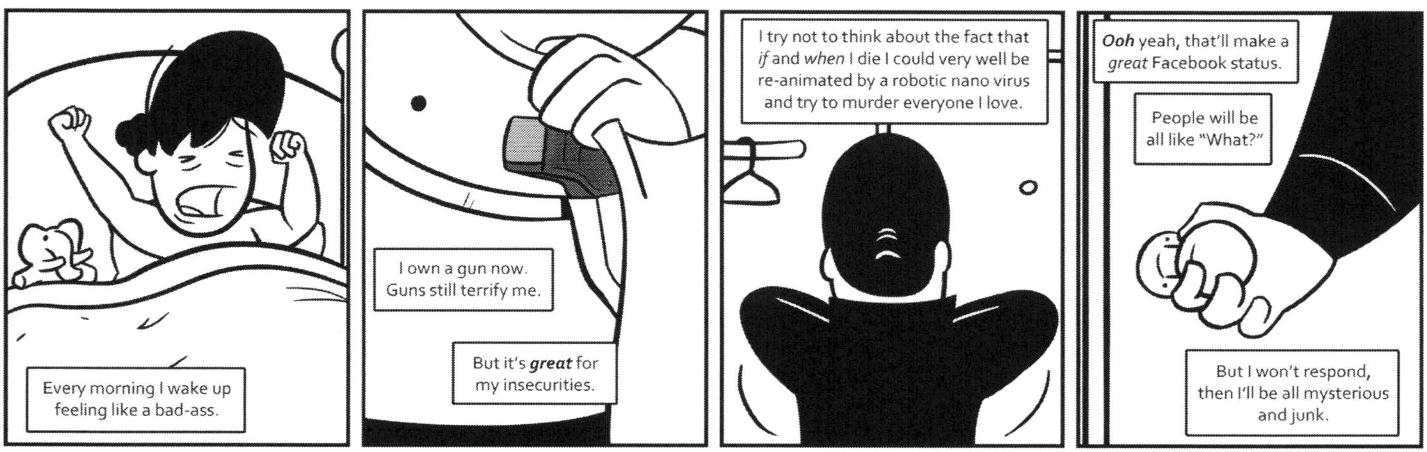

Every morning I wake up feeling like a bad-ass.
I own a gun now. Guns still terrify me.
But it's ***great*** for my insecurities.
I try not to think about the fact that *if* and *when* I die I could very well be re-animated by a robotic nano virus and try to murder everyone I love.
Ooh yeah, that'll make a *great* Facebook status.
People will be all like "What?"
But I won't respond, then I'll be all mysterious and junk.

"Illusion Dispelled"

Ok Max, I've seen you leave for work dressed like a business man *too* many times to believe you anymore. You don't really still work for ***Gassy Pumps*** do you?
...Alright no, I don't. I.. *Uh*.. I'm an accountant at *RGI Insurance* now.
The big building at the other end of town?
Are you friggin' **serious**? ***You***? When did *you* learn accounting?
What guy?
I ***know*** a guy ok!?
Just a **guy**! ***Jesus***.
Alright **fine**, but I hope you "*new job*" pays better than your old one because your half of the rent is due soon.
It ***won't*** be a problem.
That was ***so*** smooth.
404
Oh my God I'm living with a drug dealer.

"Hindenbaker Part 1"

Ooh cookies! Who are those for?
...Wade.
Really? Does he even *eat*?
Yes. Of course.
Hmm. I was *so* sure he was just like a really boring computer hologram or something.

"Hindenbaker Part 2"

*Hi **Wade!***
I baked you some cookies! Oatmeal chocolate chip.
From home?
Yes actually, I made them myself. It's kind of a hobby of mine..
Creation of food outside laboratory environment.
Increased likely-hood for contact with contagion.
No thank you.
**tikkity-takka*

"Hindenbaker Part 3"

Oh *great*! **Leftovers**! Can I have one?
It'll cost you your life.
...Alright sit down.
Thanks, anything I can do to help?
Just.. Don't be a jerk.

"Nice Of You To Ask"

Hey Max, are you *seeing* anyone right now?
I uh... *No..* ***Why***?
Because there's something I wanted to ask you to do, but it'd be no fun if you had a girlfriend.
..Look, *Dick*.. You're a *pretty* good-looking guy and all but I don't ***really***-
You wanna go to the club!? Go ***clubbin'***? *Meet some babes*?
Oh.
Sorry bro I cut you off there, wasn't listening. What were you saying?
That clubs are totally great and we should go there to meet the women.

"Gearing Up"

So what kind of stuff does one wear to a club?
Cool stuff, bro.
Let's start by gettin' rid of this tie and pop up your collar.
Now a little jewellery, *industrial strength cologne...*
..And let's undo a few buttons. Let the ladies get a **peek**.
Now, *for your hair...*
..*Ok* your hair's already pretty ridiculous.
You're good.

"Why Not Dick Mobile"

Come on bro, we'll take *my* car.
Woah! Nice car!
Yeah.. I call it the "**Banana Mobile**" Ya know, for the *ladies*.
Pff! Seriously? That's **not** sexy.
Yeah it *is*! It's suggestive as ***hell***.
Yeah, so.. You get a lot of banana in this thing?
NO. I get lots of *BABES!*
Don't you see? It's **ironic**.

"Thought He Was A Pimp"

I can't **wait** to show you 'round the clubs bro.
We're gonna ***clean up***.
We'll be rounding them ladies up **two by two**. Just like Noah's Ark.
Noah's ark had *two*-gender couples, like women **and** men, for *breeding*.
Man, whatever I never even *saw* that movie.

"Connections"

There's *no way* I'm cool enough to get into this club.
You leave that to me..
Check it, bouncer bro!
THE CLUB
Alright, head in.
Woah..
Wow! You just flashed your bureau badge! Does that work ***anywhere***?
Nah, just here. Bilge knows a guy.
Looks cool as ***hell*** though.

"Coolosity Maximus"

Here bro put these on!
SMACK
Sunglasses? But.. We're ***in**doors.*
Man where have you *been? Cool people* wear sunglasses indoors now!
Well why aren't ***you*** wearing any?
That **is** my pair bro, I'm helping *you* out. Don't look a gift bro in the mouth, bro.
-flick-
Ok now I know why cool people always look distant and brooding.. It's because they have *no God damn idea where they are.*

"Gonna Need A Radar"

Alright *good luck* buddy, I am off to pick up babes!
*You're **leaving** me??*
Don't worry you'll be fine. Trust your *instincts*. I'll be back.
Dammit Dick! I'm rolling blind here!
I need you to be my seeing-eye bro!!
Ok.. Ok don't panic. I'm **cool**. I can do this.
Look out, ladies, *here I come!*
...M-Marco?

"Stereo Sound"

NN-TSS
NN-TSS
NN-TSS
UN-TSS
UN-TSS
Hey big guy! What do you think ***you're*** doin' !?
Why are you makin' that ***noise*** with your mouth like that?
There's *already* music here bro.
Just try it bro! It's awesome. ***Way*** better.
Uuh.. *Alright*.
..Ok.
NNN
Uh..
NN-TSS!
NN-
NN-
NN-
TSS!
TSS!
TSS!
*Oh my gosh this is **super** fun.*

"The Death Tint"

Oh my God it's so *dim* in here.
I better look *really* **really** cool.
Hey **watch it** *little man!*
Sorry!
Sorry!
Oh man it's getting dangerous in here. I better head for the music, mix in with the crowd.
UN-TSS
UN-TSS
UN-TSS
Then I can stand still and let the ladies come to **me.**
WHAP

"A Vision"

Oh sorry! Are you **ok?** *Let me help you!*
Yeah it's ok, it's just these ***stupid-***
Eep!
What's the matter sweetie? *Cat's got your tongue?*
God **I hope not** because that would be the *worst possible* explanation for the erection I just got!

"Who Else But Davison"

NN-TSS
Hey big guy, I like your dancing!
UN-TSS
Thanks babe, I like your skanky clothing!
NN-TSS
Do you want to get out of here, go do something?
UN-TSS
Do I want to GO?! You think you can take me??
NN-TSS
Check out this bicep! It's like a snake choking on a watermelon!
WUB-WUB
You can't handle this!
UN-TSS
No you misheard me! I don't want to fight!
NN-TSS
Have it your way lady! Put up your dukes and let's see your best shot!

"Conversatus Interruptus"

So you seem like a pretty nice, normal guy. Maybe a *bit* out of your element though? All the guys here are kind of **big**... And ***stupid***.
I'm ***so*** glad you think so! Everytime I lay eyes on a pretty girl I blurt out something *ridiculous* and deal-breaking...
Well, I thought it was funny! ..Assuming you ***were*** joking.
Oh I ***was!*** I *totally* was!
My name is Max, by the way.
Max, I like that. Mine is-
WHAT'S UP BOUNCER BROS? **BRING IT ON**. I can dance ALL DAY.
Oh no, *no*... **Damn**.
What? The yelling? It's probably just some drunken dick.
You're *half* right.

"Hasty Exit"

Look, I *know* that guy. I have to go. I'm **so** sorry.
I will be ***right*** back.
It's dangerous to go alone.
Take this.
Call me.
Dick you ***IDIOT!*** **What are you doing?**
GRAAH!!
THE CLUB
SLAM
Bro, that was *so* much **FUN!**
-Wasn't it?
..Dude you look pissed.

"Treasure Map"

Don't be mad, buddy. I come to the club every week-
It ends the same pretty much each time.
...What? Oh.. Oh **I get it**.
Did your lady hunt turn out? Did I ***interrupt*** something bro?
Actually ***yes***, you did.
..I just never got her name.
403-
287
253

"Breaking It Down"

...So you met a girl? ***Nice!***
Not just that, ***I showed her my moves...***
*Right there in the club?! **YOU DAWG!!***
Not like that! You're disgusting.
I ***danced*** for her...
You ***dance?***
Dance is very intimate for me so..
Only.. For ***very special*** people.

WARPGOAT

"But How Cool Would That Be"

The very next day...
Hey... I'm sorry if this is too soon but I couldn't stop thinking about you.
Wait, who's this?
..Max. From the club last night?
Max eh? Hmm doesn't ring a bell. You aren't the guy I went home with are you? Because I'm pretty sure he's still in the other room...
Wh-WHAT?
Shveety, whoosh on the phone?
IS THAT SEAN CONNERY?
Wish a Dinoshaur'sh body, yesh.
The very next day ...(real life)
My dreams. Are so messed up.

"R.E.S.P.E.C.T."

Hey, can I ask you a question?
It better be about training or the Scoria threat. Because that would be relevant and **not** a waste of time.
Well actually it's-
I've contacted the FBI regarding the Scoria attacks. As two of the incidents occured *within* the US. I wanted to know if they would potentially share their findings and intelligence reports.
We don't really have a dedicated intelligence division.
I take care of that.
They sent me back an email with some irrelevant and *highly* inappropriate internet links.
Like what?
At a cursory glance they involved goats, *lemons*, ***spinning meat***. Not very helpful.
Wow those guys are **jerks**.
Well they've just never really taken us seriously.
Also they're jerks.

"Buddy Bureaus"

So *why* does the FBI hate us so much?
They don't hate us, we've actually worked together a few times before. But they're ***famous*** so they don't treat us with very much respect.
-Even though we're practically ***neighbours*** in where we operate.
So *far*, all joint operations have ended in arguments, prank-wars and there was even a ***slap fight*** one time.
But do they know anything about the attacks? Or the Scoria at all?
If they do, they aren't ready to share. We can only focus on preparation for a second attack right now.
Wow your day *sucks* doesn't it.
Yes.

"Although A Learning Experience"

Hey. I did come here to ask you a question though... How long is it normal to wait before calling a girl after you meet her?
..How in the hell did you get my phone number?
No! Not you, a girl I met at a club last night!
Listen, I have no idea. I don't date. Ask someone else.
Well it looks like coming up here was a big waste of time...
Undoubtedly and for EVERYONE INVOLVED!

"Here We Go"

Attention! Attention Maxworth!
Maxmillion.
Maxilarissimo.
Was that thing there a moment ago?
Shh! It s Bilge.
My boy, I'd have you report to my office sharpish.
We have business.
DOG
HUMAN
Also, bring a butterfly net. A really rather big one.
-As though you were going to try to catch a very large, hairy butterfly.
With horns.

"Not Skeletons"

Oh *jolly good!* You found a suitable net.
Yeah there was one in the tool shed on the forty-second floor.
Director Bilge
There was also *some*... Kind of **weird** stuff in there too.
Some of it was ***monogrammed?***
Director Bilge
-cough-
Anyway I need you to catch the **Warpgoat**.
What.

"Legacy"

Catching the Warpgoat is an old initiation task of our institution...
But what ***is*** a "Warpgoat"?
Well it's bloody well a ***goat***, isn't it?
It is ***also*** an inter-dimensional being of *immense power*.
Quite docile, mind you! At first appearances it is nothing more than a goat who is also a snappy dresser.
But this *particular* goat possesses the ability to move through time and space on a singular *goaty whim*.
Hurry now, the Warpgoat comes and goes as it pleases. Haven't the foggiest why it likes to visit us but it's been spotted in the thirty-sixth floor lunch room.
But how do you ***catch*** something like that?
It is the **ultimate** test of patience and perseverance.
But seeing as no one has ever *completed* the task, I am mostly making that up.
I ***won't*** let you down, sir!
Director Bilge
You very well might but good luck anyway my boy!

"Anticipation"

Bilge said that no other agent of the bureau had *ever* caught the Warpgoat.
DING!
I was soon to learn this was **not** for lack of trying.
LUNCH ROOM
LUNCH WILL NOT BE PROVIDED
heh-
heh!

"Goat Spotting"

Bilge's intel was spot on. Warpgoat was indeed where he said.
-wring-
I was *excited.*
There it was.
Munchin' on a table.
-sneak-
So ***majestic.***
CRUNCH
MUNCH
-admire-

"Swing And A Miss"

AAAAAAAAAAAAH
Was it *arrogance* or *confidence* that made me strike without hesitation?
-SHVOOM-
WHOOOSH
Didn't matter.
To be fair, I ***was*** warned about this.

"Whoosh Swish Whoosh"

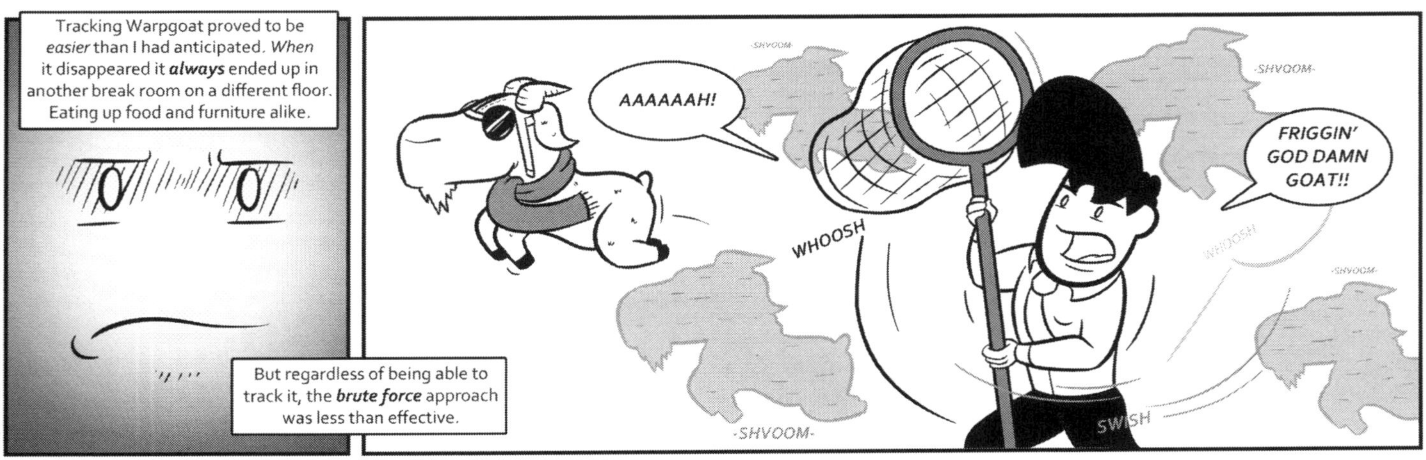
Tracking Warpgoat proved to be *easier* than I had anticipated. *When* it disappeared it ***always*** ended up in another break room on a different floor. Eating up food and furniture alike.
But regardless of being able to track it, the ***brute force*** approach was less than effective.
AAAAAAAH!
-SHVOOM-
FRIGGIN' GOD DAMN GOAT!!
WHOOSH
SWISH

"Multilingual"

I had to change up my tactics. The next time I came face to face with Warpgoat, I attempted to communicate with it.
ahem Erm... **Baah**.
Results were... Inconclusive.
*Maach-Baah-**Bleat!***
MREEEAAAHHHH!
Some time later...
Mreah! *Maah, BAH* ***BLEAT-BAAH!!***
I DON'T KNOW *WHY* YOU HAVE TO BRING MY INCOME INTO THIS, YOU **KNOW** I WORK HARD FOR MY THINGS!

"Handy Man"

Warpgoat made light of my traps and surprises.
-SHVOOM-
BLEAT!
!
Warpgoat was everywhere.
THWUNK
-SHVOOM-
*...And yet **nowhere**.*
Good grief.

"Enlisting Services"

At one point I even considered enlisting the aid of a *bounty hunter* of sorts.
Using the internet I managed to find a self-proclaimed "***Goat Lover***".
I figured that if *anyone* knew about goat taming, it would be this guy.
Although when he *arrived*.. it became apparent that we ***may*** have misinterpreted eachother.
I
Goats
The problem solved itself however, for when the '***Goat Lover***' attempted to '***make contact***' with Warpgoat, Warpgoat warped *away*, reportedly seen outside the window of the *fifty-first floor...*
Yet Warpgoat returned ***alone***.
Immediately I returned to what I had been doing, whistling nonchalantly and not seeing ***anything***.
-Just as I had been doing all afternoon. *That's my story and It makes sense* ***alright what are you a cop?***

"Warplunch"

The Warpgoat had driven me to *wit's end*. I was on the verge of giving up, like so many others before me.
Well, there were *three or four* people before. But still, ***they*** all gave up.
But later, at lunch-
-Right as that ***jackass*** warped in *just* to take a bite of *my* sandwich...
Inspiration struck!
CRUNCH
MUNCH
I could not ***go*** to Warpgoat, it would have to come to ***me***.
But now I knew exactly what it wouldn't be able to resist.

"Ace In The Hole"

Goats will try to eat almost anything. It's just how they are.
But there was clearly something *special* about my sandwich.
tikkity-takka
How had I not thought of it sooner? The ultimate bait. *It was so obvious.*
Goat cheese.
Yes, *goat cheese*. Why? You ask? **Simple**.
Their kind produces the raw ingredients for this delicacy their *entire lives*, but they have neither the knowledge nor the means to produce it!
SCIENCE
It is an unattainable dish to the ***entire species!***
What?
Don't look at me like that.
It *was* ***too*** a good idea!

"Alleyoop"

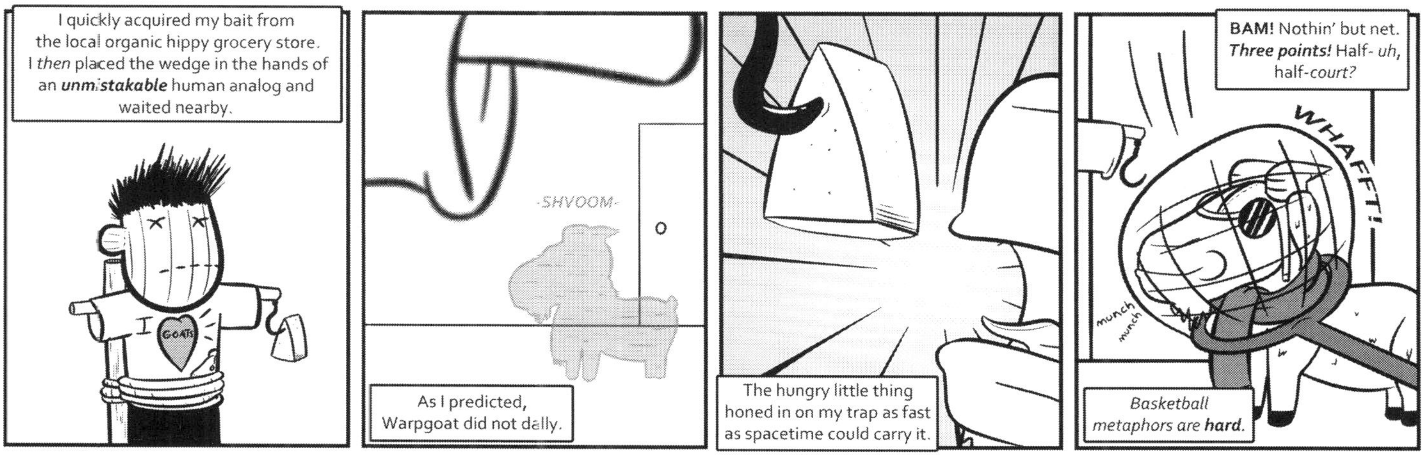
I quickly acquired my bait from the local organic hippy grocery store. I *then* placed the wedge in the hands of an ***unmistakable*** human analog and waited nearby.
I GOATS
-SHVOOM-
As I predicted, Warpgoat did not dally.
The hungry little thing honed in on my trap as fast as spacetime could carry it.
BAM! Nothin' but net. ***Three points!*** Half- *uh*, half-*court?*
WHAFFT!
munch munch
*Basketball metaphors are **hard**.*

"Remorse"

You may, *at this point*, be wondering why Warpgoat did not simply ***warp away***.
And *no*, it was ***not*** a "magic net" or anything silly like that.
In actuality Warpgoat is just a good sportsman who ***respects*** the *rectitude* of competition.
I think.
Woo! *Suck on **that**, probability!*
But as I gazed upon one of evolution's *most **scruffy-wuffiest*** chinned creatures…
I froze up.
What was I supposed to **do** with this thing anyway? ***Ride it to Bilge's office?***
No.
I knew what I had accomplished. Warpgoat would go free.

"Jeepers Creepers"

Before I could release Warpgoat, I had to look it in the eye, and tell it I was *sorry*.
Man, goats have such ***weird*** eyes.
Wha-*agh*-***AAHH!!*** ***Everything's sideways!!***
Good lord help me, I'm SIDEWAYS BLIND!!!
SHVOOM
WHUMP

"Residual Tendencies"

Director Bilge. *I did it*. I *caught* the Warpgoat...
Bloody brilliant my boy! But you look *distraught*, whatever did you end up *doing* with it?
I let it go. So I *don't* have any proof.
Well did you ***learn*** anything from the experience?
Yes. Before letting it go, I looked *straight* into its eyes...
I was temporarily *blinded* but I saw... *What I saw was..*
I saw ***everything.***
It left an imprint on my ***soul.***
I may now know ***every single thing*** there is to know about goats.
And scarves.
That is ***fascinating!*** I'd *heard* of this phenomenon before, only, with ***other*** kinds of *warping animals...*
I believe you and Warpgoat may now share a ***mental link*** of sorts.
Hah! Same thing happened to myself once with a **walrus**. But we both ended up regretting it and had it annulled shortly after...
Ah.
Neat, listen.
tap
tap
For some reason I **really** want to gnaw on this desk right now.
Have at it.
You don't mind?
Not at all.

A MARVELOUS MAN

The legend of Thomas Bilge

At the tip-toppest up-most of the fifty-first floor,
worked a man men and women alike did adore.

And there on his face, rooted right into place,
was a winterous, wonderous mous-tache.

Truly a marvelous man.

The best thing about him, was that no-one could tout him,
as having lost to them in fisticuff-bouts.

A brawler, enthraller and quite a bit taller,
than other, less-marvelous men.

The praise stretched for days were it written all down,
but the story can change when there's no-one around.

Try never to let his sights-set on a drink,
lest you wish to see fists fly as fast as thoughts think.

In slumber beneath un-assuming knit-sweater,
waits a rippling man-beast, a brute and a better.

A warning, that is only, do not think old Bilge evil.
In fact he's aligned with the chaotic-good people.

Just quicker to scrap once potion meets lips,
preferring knuckles to well-rehearsed Brit-accented quips.

Still quite a marvelous man.

Now back to the good stuff, of which there's a lot!
Bilge founded the ground on which we now trot.

The Aversion Bureau, who make saving roll-throw,
when the phone rings and peril is there-

With financing options, for those out-of-pocket,
your preferred brand of justice? Surely they stock it!

Oh my, what a marvelous man!

SNOWDOWN

"With All The Amenities"

Nestled deeply in the North-Eastern reaches of the Rocky Mountains,
hides a ***top secret*** Aversion Bureau training facility.
And right there, *right now*, ***things*** are happening.
Also **stuff**...
Hey! ***Ouch!***
WHOPT

"Spar Me The Details"

JAB
HOOK
DUCK
OOF!
UPPERCUT

"What Were The Odds"

HOP
THOK
STUMBLE..
Oh my God I'm *so dead*.

"The Ante Is Up"

OH MY GOD I'M SO SORRY.
Stone I'm so, **so** sorry!
So-so-SO-SO SORRY!
DUST
BRUSH
It was just a reflex! I didn't think there was **any** way I would ***actually*** hit you!
I mean, I *uh-*
FLING!
What?
SCHWIP
Oh HELL no!
Ok you win! ***You win!***
Just be cool-

"Truly 'Tis A Talent"

Why did you bring me out to this *God-forsaken* waste anyway?
To implement *exposure to the elements* as a facet of your training. Fighting in the cold builds character.
Couldn't we have just trained back at headquarters?
-Additionally
I was **sure** that the lower temperatures would *limit* your ability to complain.
Oh my dear, you ***never cease*** to underestimate me.

"A Little Inconvenient"

YAWN
So what's the plan for ***today?*** Naps. I hope.
Long-barrelled weapons training. Follow me.
Hey, *listen,* it's been a **day** already and I haven't eaten *anything.*
I've been too *scared* to ask you if you brought any food but now I can't take it anymore. I'm ***starving.***
Your question could not have come at a more appropriate time.
There *just so happens* to be a ***delicious*** ham and cheese bagel tied to a post in that clearing.
OH MY GOD.
You ***totally*** suck!

"Bagel Tease"

Look, a hungry forest critter has been attracted by the scent of your ward.
Sniff
Sniff
Right on time, too.
Here is the rifle. **Defend your bagel.**
I - I uh.
But I don't ***want*** to shoot the deer!
Are you not ***hungry?***
Yes, ***but!***
Quickly now! That bagel is *especially* delicious to a deer.
SMOOSH
Deer ***love*** ham.

"Down To The Wire"

Time's running out, Mr. Martin. *Take the shot.*
I don't want to!
Take the shot, protect your lunch.
Don't make me do this!
That deer just *licked* your bagel. Rescue it from sustaining further ***deer germs.***
I don't want it this way!
Pull the trigger, Max.
Damn it!
BANG
THWIP
?
-*Wait.* ***Training markers?*** What the ***hell?***
It was a test of your ability to perform under pressure.
Congratulations. You did *alright.*

"Emergence"

Aww *look at it*, it's havin' a little breakfast.
...You ***did*** bring more food though, right?
munch munch
RUMBLE...
Yes.
Thank **God**.
CRASH
PLUCK!

"A Fairly Obvious Plan"

Yeti. Run.
tap
RAAOOOAWR
Where are we running?!
Back to the cabin!
Shh! Not so loud! He's gonna hear you!

"The Getaway"

Wait! I still have the gun! Did you bring any real ammo?
No.
CREAK
Are you serious? Well what DO we have?
A sled.
What use is a
JUST GET ON THE DAMN SLED.
FWOOOOSH
Hands on the shoulders, agent.
Sorry.

"High Octane"

Looks like gravity's on our side today, if we can just *outpace* him, we can call Davison for evac.
Look I don't mean to sound cliche', **but:**
RAVINE!
Woohoo! *We are badasses!*
FWOoosh

"Friction On Vacation"

CRASH
!
SWIPE
Swish
Swipe
SWISH
SLIP
Shoosh
Yes!
No!

"Boy What A Cheap Gun"

I got this.
FUMBLE!
slap
Fwump
Uh oh.
BANG
Uh, yeah! That's right, stay down.

"Suddenly An Opinion"

Phew.
Good work. I'll get Davison on the line.
Alright, that tears it. When we get home, I'm finally calling that girl from the club. Clearly I'm living on borrowed time.
You still haven't called her? How long has it been?
A week.
Wow, you should probably have called her by now.

Scales And Justice

A mission remembered. By Natalie Stone.

The night was cloudy and cold. **My favourite weather.** What are stars, anyway?

A light source. A luxury I prefer not to allow my prey.

I approached my targets in the night, satchels and scabbards strapped silently to my form. Amongst my equipment, a twenty-five inch black katana. **Zeratul.** He is as much a part of my body as my own arm. Thin branches cluttering the forest floor remained intact as I moved over them. I am a ghost. I am the literal and physical reaper made legend by virtue of reality.

That night I was after a group, were they not already heavily established in the area, that I would consider easy enough for even agent *Martin* to deal with. Unfortunately this operation had flown under the radar for long enough that the mission required.. ***ordinance***. I'll get to that in a moment. The target was a sect of the order of the Obsidian Fin, an old, but un-forgotten enemy of the bureau. Not to dive into any etymology, but these abominations are essentially bi-pedal fish men. Allowed to walk and breathe on land by crude environmental suits which equate to fish-bowl helmets in constant need of re-filling and frequent trips to a bathing station,
lest the wearer get too dry.

The collective intelligence of the entire fish-man race would lose a game of Family Feud to a wrist watch calculator in any given technological period. That is not a whimsical statement, it is the result of a clinical trial.

No GPS required that night. My feet met with a familiar crisp as they reached the ground approaching a clearing in the foliage. **Fish flakes.** I was getting close. The greatest thing about the absurd excuse for technology that allows the fish-men to exist on land is that their bowls reflect moonlight like bulls-eye disco balls. Two guards were standing at the edge of the clearing, facing inwards. *Towards* the compound. Why.

I silently approached the left-most guard and tapped the glass of his helmet-bowl. They hate it when you do that.

As it turned around to face the disturbance, the pommel of my katana found crunchy purchase on the smooth glass of its breathing bowl. Glass bowls. They aren't even trying. One swift movement leaves the second guard in one more piece than it had been but moments before. The game was on now; I paced quickly towards the centre of the compound.

Then, a *mistake*. In my haste and lowered guard, I had stepped too close to a watch tower reminiscent construct, that was.. *too pathetic to describe.* My form melted into shadow while I waited for the alerted guard to convince himself that I was nothing more than a whisper from the forest. No need to wait long however, one lap around the viewing platform it was watching from and a neutral expression returned to that moist, vacant face. Fish memories. **Hysterical**.

Although incredibly inept and sensually-inferior, fish-men carry sepsis inducing harpoon shotguns. Something that it is not wise to draw attention from if it isn't necessary to do so. My mission then nearly completed itself when I came mere inches from a rigid, invisible structure blocking further progress into the camp. Problem solved, as this was the target. A fish-tank fortress over five storeys high, sitting in the forest, towering above a good deal of the surrounding foliage and kept hidden during the day with an enormous tarp depicting a scene of that same patch of forest as if there *weren't* a grotesquely obvious lair situated there.

I just do not understand fish-men.

In the murky waters of the tank I could see sleeping warriors, floating ghost-like in the dark. Eyelids that are never there create an eerie illusion of ever-watchfulness. I work quickly to solve the problem. A C4 explosive satchel set to a minute long timer is affixed to the outside of the glass before I ready my shoe laces for a healthy sprint to safety. As the red warning light on the satchel charge blinks monotonously, the figures of many more fish-men are illuminated. A high-score, surely.

Before I leave I make sure to tap the glass loudly and clearly. They really hate it. That night the sky glittered with an eruption of atomized water, powdered glass and very, very poor ideas.

RELOAD
SAVE

"So Close"

Here we go-
I'm home,
I'm *determined*.
It is time to
call that girl.
SPACE QUEST 3
Hold on.
SAVE SPACE
I am the hero
this galaxy ***deserves***.
SAVE SPACE

"Where Has The Time Gone"

Well I'll just start playing a little to *calm my nerves*, maybe get some confidence back.
Call her in a little bit.
50 hours later.
I HAVE NO STRENGTH OF WILL AND I HAVE COME TO ACCEPT THIS.

"Spin The Wheel"

No! I can't put it off any longer! What am I *thinking?*
This is it!
*beep boop
I am calling this woman ***right now!***
*What the **hell?***
BZZZz
Hello?
cough
Hi! It's Max.
This is the call service. You requested to be woken up at *sexy o'clock?*
Do you know what time it is?!
Uh...
cough
Hi! It's Max.
This is the call service. You requested to be woken up at *sexy o'clock?*

"In The Headlights"

CAUTION:
BREATH VOLUME INCREASING
BREATHING VOLUME CRITICAL
SITUATION IS NOW CREEPY.
ABORT!!!
SMASH
TOSS
MISSION FAILED
Retry?
WHOMP

"Sometimes It's Why"

What's wrong Max? You've hardly **touched** the marshmallows in your cereal this morning.
Marshmallows are for winners.
Are you ***joking?*** Losers eat marshmallows all the time! *Especially* at your age. It's not exactly the *'breakfast of champions'*.
In fact, marshmallows belong to a food group that champions specifically avoid. ***Not food***.
Marshmallows are not even food.
Wow yeah, you're right! ***Thanks!***

THE BORING MEN

"Think Fast"

URGENT! REQUEST FOR AID
RE: SWARM OF MURDER DUCKS
Agent Martin, you may remember
Regards, Bill.
Grumble...
Maxston! *Quickly!* *Hide this booze!*

"Better Than Some Places"

Wait what? Bilge? Hide it?
Whoosh
FOR THE LOVE OF GOD DO IT NOW!!
...Bilge? Everything all right in here?
Absolutely lovely my dear.

"Spit Shine"

I thank you for your excellent work, my boy.
Truly you are a quick thinker.
In fact, this prompts me to believe you may be perfect for a special assignment.
A mission of utmost importance!
Well I'm honoured sir, but I'm a little concerned that this mission will end up with me being shot at by law enforcement while attempting to transport large amounts of liquor illegally.
Oh my no! Nothing so crass, agent! This is an organization dedicated to protecting the world after all.
Besides. Hiding the occasional mickey in an orifice or two more than exceeds your requirements in that field.

"The Breakdown"

I need you to deliver a briefcase to some, *"friends"* of the bureau. ***The boring men***.
They operate from the basement of the *Beige Dollar casino* downtown.
CASINO
BEIGE
DOLLAR
You must very simply gain entry with your badge, then leave the case with their leader and return without turning any heads.
You will do *fine*, I am sure of it.
Bilge, this all sounds very.. ***sinister***.
I will admit, it is **not** my *proudest* association. But it is very important, nonetheless.
I don't want to let you down.
Lad, in your brief time here, you have proven yourself ***much*** more competent than one would think just by looking at you.
T-Thank you.
That was from ***the heart.***

"First Warning"

I have a lot of faith in you, agent. But I suggest you get going.
It's been a long day and I am about to become phenominally drunk. ***Halloween*** *drunk*.
THIRSTY OLD BASTARD
Ha ha! Oh, ***Bilge!***
Ok I'm leaving.
Good man.

“Wise Words”

That evening...
CASINO
BEIGE
DOLLAR
My mother always used to say that casinos were where the devil goes to steal your money.
She said the same thing about non-christian charities and movies, every time a new Adam Sandler comedy came out.
Well she was right about one thing.

“Nice Enough Place”

Oh, ***wow!*** It’s like *Where’s Waldo* but with ***gambling addicts!***
Except that it’s *really easy* because they’re ***everywhere!***
..**Actually** I have *no idea* where I was going with that.
But hey, ***wow!***

"To Be Fair"

Man, Bilge did **not** explain this very well. **"The boring men"**, was it?
*I guess I just look for the most **boring** person around...*
But I suppose that's open to interpretation.

"Not Well Hidden"

VIP
...Hold on.
It's gotta be ***those*** guys. The big one looks **really** boring.
Gentlemen.
Right this way..
*Pfft. **Friggin' rank fours.***

"The Basement"

What the *hell* did that guy **mean?** ***Rank four?!***
What's a *'rank four'* anyway?
His ***mom's*** a rank four.
At sex.
-*Wow* what are these guys, like *twins* or something?
Starting to get a *little* uneasy here...
Woah. Well this.. **Not as nice.**
And this is... *Weird*.. ***Everyone looks exactly the same***.
..And they all look so ***bored***.
Oh. I think I get it now!
SNAP

"Run On Thought"

Uh - thanks for escorting me over big guy!
I'm sure I couldn't have found the only door in the entire dingy-basement-slot machine hangar labelled "Office" on my own.
Holy hell. Even their leader is identical!
Are they all robots?
Why would they be called "The boring men" if they were robots?
Robots are cool!
Except for those ones that were doing all that murder on the beach.
Those robots were jerks. Robo-jerks.
Robots should only exist to fetch us things from the fridge.
God I should shut up.

"What's On The Inside"

Excuse me? Hello, hi. I'm agent Martin from the Aversion Bureau, I was told-
To...
ZZzzziiip
Fwump!
Greetings.

"Please Be Serious"

What's the matter, agent Martin? Looks like you've seen a ghost.
BWA HAHA HAHAHAAAAAA!
Hoo-HOO-boy! I'm hilarious.
God damn.
Who are you?
My name is unpronounceable in your language.
Really?
Nope. That was a bit of generic fantasy bullshit. I just don't want to tell you.
HAH!

Z Z Z

"The Shadow Broker"

Ah *yes*, the *bribe money*. I **knew** you couldn't just be here to feel the force of my ***wicked jokes***.
Bribe money? I never looked inside, I- *what?*
Oh? You don't know...
Oh.. *No* ***no***. Of *course* you don't!
You're just a ***new one.***
-Why does Bilge give you money?
Naked pictures of your dad!
..Seems like a *bit much* doesn't it.
No no no... We are ***information brokers***, my people.
We have ***many*** underworld connections, literally *being* from another realm beneath the crust of the earth ourselves.
Simple information brokers keeping *your* organization informed on the activities of many sub-humans and a few *other-wordly* races.
These, ***husks***, allow us to blend in with your people and more easily work the slots.
Well, I suppose that doesn't seem ***so*** bad..
Oh no, it really isn't, yet your director is ***so*** *ashamed of us.*
Probably *because you're a* ***demon ghost*** *living in a* ***mansuit***.
The fact that you're dwelling on this makes it clear you haven't been working for the bureau ***very long***.

"Nope"

And so now that you more fully understand the legitimacy of our operation... Perhaps you can *lighten up a bit?*
I suppose...
The basement floor may be wall to wall slot machines *right now*. But every other Sunday we ***push 'em*** to the walls, *clear out some room..*
And just do some ***weird stuff.***
SMACK
Bye.
Thanks for the cash, meatdancer.

"Intersection"

God, no *wonder* Bilge said he wasn't proud of this deal. These guys are totally messed up.
Friggin' ***pervert ghost***.
SMACK
THUD!
*Gosh-****DAMN IT*** *Terry!* I ***told you*** to fasten the little clip things!
I ***did*** *fasten the clip things, they just suck!*
Clearly you DID NOT fasten the little clip things Terry!

"Red Handed"

Greg you **always** put me down. *I* ***know*** *I made a* ***mistake*** *ok?*
But Terry you ***ALWAYS*** *do thi-*
Wait.
THE HUMAN!
Yo ***Zipperteeth!*** This doesn't look like "*simple information*" to ***me!***
OFFICE
!
Kill him.

"Good News"

Oh ***God*** *I hope this thing works just like a* ***regular*** *gun...*
Terry, ***tell me*** you remembered to take the ammo out of that gun in the case.
PEW-Chu!
Terry don't give me that loo-
DAMN IT TERRY ARE YOU SERIOUSLY KIDDING ME?!?

"Forward Down Down Forward Punch"

EXIT
SLAM
BOUND!
FWUMP
Terry?
K.O.

"It Looked Suspicious"

Ok.
What are you?
Ya serious kid?
We gotta leave!
-Fine. Agent Whiskers. Aversion Bureau field agent. Black ops.
No. Seriously.
There's a lot of outrageous crap going on right now.
Seriously pal. That's the truth. It's just yer luck I was upstairs investigatin' when ya walked in.
I saw ya headin' down, figured who you was and kept an ear out.
Investigating what?
A Blackjack table.
It's...
ongoing.

"The Cavalry"

Useless God damn devil-guys...
Men! Arm yourselves! No survivors.
PLUNGE
Pull!
Grab!
EQU
Don't suppose *you* keep a sword in *your* back, eh kid?
Nope.
Well **damn**.

"Let The Light In"

PADDA-PADDA
PEW PEW!
Thwip
Thwip
Thwip

"Escaping The Basement"

They won't stop coming! *What do we do?*
Well ***I'd say*** we kick ass *back-to-back* 'til we *win* or ***die***.
But I sense yeh probably don't got the stones for ***that***.
CHOP
A-hah! *Suck on devil-gun!*
CLICK! —CLICK!
Damn it! *Out already?*
DROPKICK
Too many! ***Just run!***
xit

“Steve McQueen Could Learn From Us”

VIP
Guh.. My face...
VIP
SMACK!
Hey! Careful, big-hair dude.
Sorry!
Bump
I'm not.
Come on! I parked right out front!
SLAM
Quickly! Hit the pedal!
What are you talking about? You're driving.
Yeah but I just think it would be really cute if you did it!

"Metagame"

Several minutes later...
Wow! That was close eh? I can't believe we-
?
Agent Whiskers? Wait, where the hell-
CR-ANK
SPIN!
PAT-PAT-WHACK PAT

"Reporting Back"

The very next morning.
RGI
...Hey reception lady, is it just me.. or
...Space pants.
Sexy.
Oh forget it I'm too tired to do this.
Shuffle
Shuffle
Swipe
BEEP!

"Admission"

51 floors later...
DING!
Shoof
THUD
Maxbert! Are you alright?
No shh. Sh-shh. Quiet.
-You suck.

"Makes Sense Now"

Director Bilge... I'm sorry that it ended like that. I know you trusted me with this assignment...
It is more than alright lad! Mostly I am glad that you made it back alive! In fact, your lucky timing caught our supposed allies nipple-deep in their double-dealing deceit!
And while their information was useful, it is now clear that dealing with the demon-ghost intel-peddling false-men was a bad idea from the start!
DUUUUUUUH.

"Still A Sad Story"

We're both ***very lucky*** that *Agent Whiskers* was at the casino that night.
You mean you really ***didn't*** send him to keep an eye on me?
Director Bilge
Heavens ***no,*** it's nearly **impossible** to tell that crazy little bugger what to do.
So he ***really was*** there just gambling.
I'm afraid so. Poor bloke's lost a marriage to it once already.
Wow *is that true?*
Well his "*wife*" was actually just an anxiety-induced multiple personality disorder.
But he still came and slept over for a few nights after the divorce to watch movies and drink irresponsibly.

"Rich In Mustache Tickles"

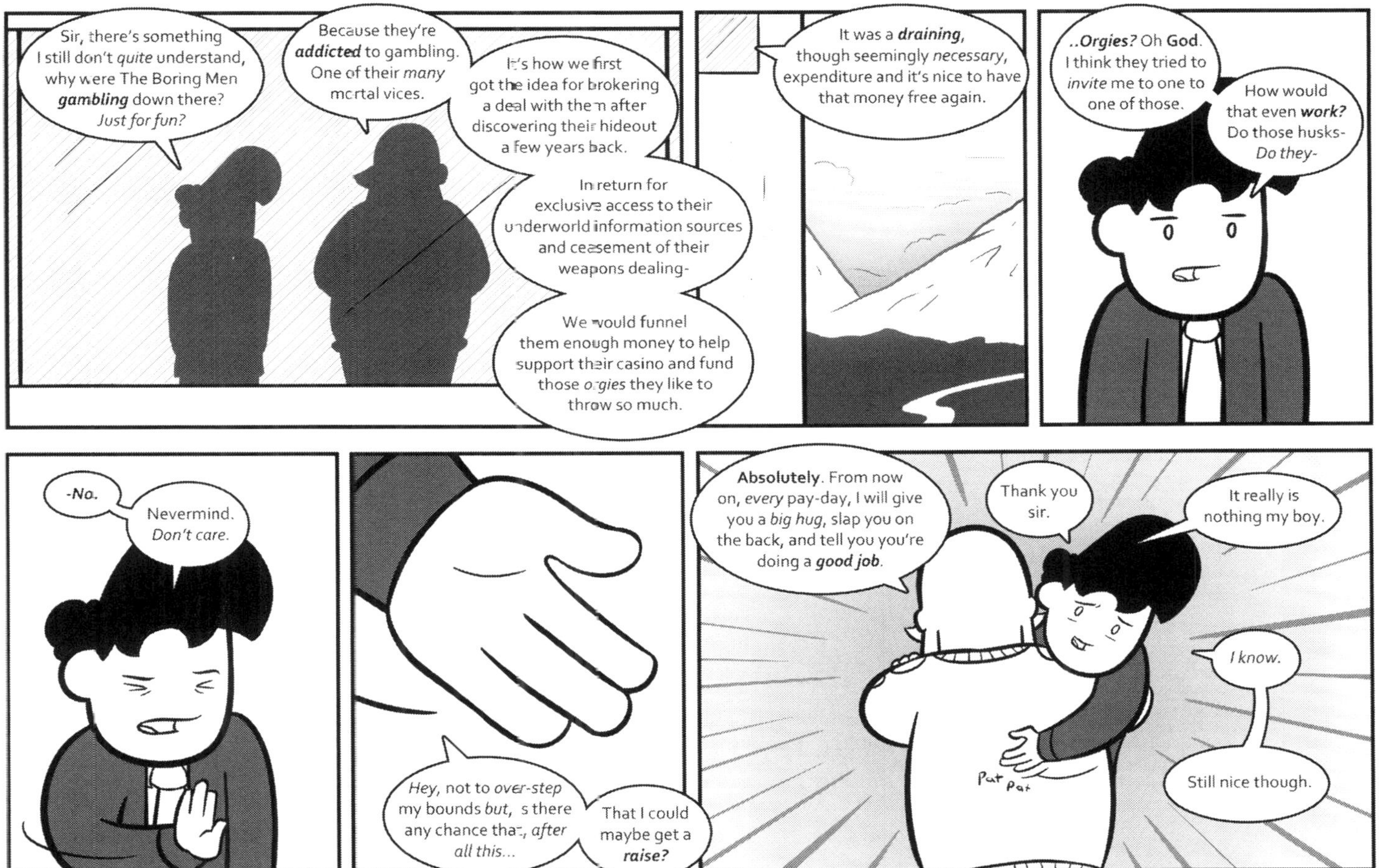

Sir, there's something I still don't *quite* understand, why were The Boring Men **gambling** down there? *Just for fun?*
Because they're **addicted** to gambling. One of their *many* mortal vices.
It's how we first got the idea for brokering a deal with them after discovering their hideout a few years back.
In return for exclusive access to their underworld information sources and ceasement of their weapons dealing-
We would funnel them enough money to help support their casino and fund those *orgies* they like to throw so much.
It was a ***draining***, though seemingly *necessary*, expenditure and it's nice to have that money free again.
..*Orgies?* Oh **God**. I think they tried to *invite* me to one to one of those.
How would that even ***work?*** Do those husks- *Do they-*
-No.
Nevermind. *Don't care.*
Hey, not to *over-step* my bounds *but,* is there any chance that, *after all this...*
That I could maybe get a ***raise?***
Absolutely. From now on, *every* pay-day, I will give you a *big hug*, slap you on the back, and tell you you're doing a ***good job***.
Thank you sir.
It really is nothing my boy.
I know.
Still nice though.
Pat Pat

BROTHER HENS

"Trickery And Deceit"

Boss-bro, *look*, when you asked me to come out for a walk today.. I was *kinda* thinking you actually wanted to hang out...
Not just lug a damn *couch* that you "*purchased from a chap on the internet*" **ten blocks** down the street and back to the bureau.
Oh, well you see, I *mislead* you. Really I just needed help with the couch.
Yeah, well. It makes sense ***now***.
I'm glad.

"Where There's A Will"

-And when I said "This will never fit in the elevator" I meant "Let's ditch it in the lobby."
Not "Let's take the stairs instead!"
But I must have it in my office! It will be the perfect combination of 'comfort' and 'in my office'.
Finally!
SMACK
Just set it down anywhere.
Thank you.
Aaaahhhh... That's comfortable.
FLOP
Davison are you also feeling this hard, bulbous form beneath the cushion?
Oh DAMN IT Bilge! It's a body isn't it? That's why it was so heavy!
This is what you get for buying a fifty-dollar yard couch!

"The Only Explanation"

Greetings human males.
Wom
wom
I am known as Skreel, of the great and former interstellar hive world collective Faa'rthgrax.
Wom
wom
Agent Davison, are we... Are we on high?
I'm not. Are you?
Sober as a nunnery.
Maybe the couch... Is made of drugs?!
Quick! I need a long-sleeve shirt!!
Rub

"A Royal Plea"

My people are dying. I am the larval form of my species sent here by one of our last queens in an attempt to safely reach adulthood away from the conflicts of our home worlds.
An odd melding of fate and targeting brought me to this furniture here today.
My life now rests in your hands.
Wom
Wom
Prior to your purchase of this cushioned buttocks-recepticle, my pod was kept warm by frequent intercourse conducted above me.
Gross.
My metamorphosis is nearly complete. I require no more than one additional solar cycle of incubation.
Wom
I must retreat to the warmth of the cushion.
SMOOSH
Please take pity on my race and remain here to birth me.

"The Couch Manoeuvre"

So. It's a sleepover then. *Uh*... How we gonna *do* this?
Feet to feet and an arm-rest each, or the best workable alternative.
We ***will*** overcome uncomfortable adversity.
A graceful and epic dance ensued...
Bilge.
Yes?
This isn't comfortable.
Stay strong, lad! ***This is for the Faa'rthgraxian people!***
Apparently.

"Or A Pillow Fight"

Bro I have *no idea* what I would do if you were a girl- that's a **weird** question.
But I *guess*, if you ***were*** a girl, I'd fantasize about doin' it with you but then eventually repel you with my over-bearing false bravado.
Standard procedure, eh? **Interesting**. Well as you know I'm a *bit old* to date.
So I will channel agent Martin and answer you as a ***young person***.
-Davison, if **you** were a girl, I would add you on a social-networking platform completely randomly one day.
And **exactly** one afternoon later, ***bolstered*** *by the shroud of faceless interaction-*
-send you a disturbingly long message professing my deepest emotions expecting *immediate* and ***total*** reciprocation.
***Aw**, that's sweet.*
But why don't they ever thinks so!?

"I Was A Fool To Deny The Blanket"

Agent Davison, *do you fear the night?*
At home, with all my guns, I fear ***no*** bro.
But *uh*.. not packin' right now so... **Kinda**.
Ah, I too face these problems from time to time, knowing full well what often lurks in the inky blackness.
But here, on the fifty-first floor of a relatively isolated towering building, my mind is at ease.
For that matter, have you ever seen a *zombie* who could work an *elevator?* **Preposterous!**
A ***Dracula*** could.
Bloody hell.

"Wiggle Twist Shuffle"

BLINK
blink
rustle
rustle
rustle
rustle
Tap
Tap
rustle
rustle
Bulge!

"But We Loved Him Anyway"

EXPL-
-ODE
SKREEEEE!!
CRASH!!!
It's beautiful.
Sniff They grow up so darn fast don't they?
SKREEE!
-Woah bro. Don't give me the "Let's kiss now" look. We went over this at that 2008 Christmas party.
You're right sorry.

"Old Yeller"

Wow, our little bro-ling has sure taken an interest in that passing, single-engine passenger aircraft...
Oh my..
Hungry fella.
Well uh... Should we go get some guns then?
We'd be murderers not to!
FIN.

What Is It Like To Be A Cat

The Agent Whiskers story

What is it like to be a cat? Let me tell ya, kid, it aint no picnic at the topless park.

Except that it is. Only **better.** Imagine that eh?

Don't have to, *livin' it.*

I wake up whenever I want to, if I'm sleeping, it's because the world doesn't need me yet. Sometimes the world doesn't need me for 16 to 18 hours at a time. ***When*** I wake up I look in the mirror, and I see a **champion**. Everyone else sees a *participant.* A saucer of bourbon and milk greets me for breakfast. I start the day hard, and my enemies know this.

An average 24-hour stretch for a boss like me is mostly spent doin' my job, 'cause my job is awesome. If ya ever spent a weekend downtown beating up loan sharks for leads on other-worldly smuggling rings, you'd know what I mean. Nobody ever suspects the cat.

I don't drive, drivin's for gangly chumps who can reach the pedals. I take the bus. I'm not just handsome, I'm environmentally conscious. *Hey ladies.* Ya ever met a bus driver that wouldn't let a kitty-cat ride for free? I have. Those are the ones with the scars.

When I arrive in "*the mission zone*" as I like to call it, I find my target with my superior cat senses

(ie : street smarts and lots of brain) and once I do find them, I like to stalk them for a while to gather intel. I walk where *they* walk, I eat when *they* eat and I nap when *they* nap. Sometimes I nap when they do other things too. I work hard alright?

I once was charged with discovering and disrupting the meeting location of an up-and-coming cult.

Ya know, one of them fancy "*we're gonna revive an ancient, impossible monster and meld it with the horrors of technology today*" ones. Turned out the bastard I needed to shadow liked eating fish!

He also liked saucers of milk, long naps and ground meat drowned in gravy, straight from the can! Turned out the guy I was supposed to watch was **me**. *I knew everything all along!* That was a good week.

When a reconnaissance assignment occasionally hits a snag or starts to take too long, I lose focus. Birds are tweeting, I want them dead. The wind is displacing my whiskers and balance is impossible.

Debris is constantly *shifting* slightly... Gravel, leaves, the sound is deafening. THAT DAMN BAG MOVED! IS IT ***ALIVE?!*** I murder it to be sure. I'm seeing movement in the concrete! **Impossible!** Anything that dangles in my vicinity does not dangle for long.

My sense are overloading from stagnation.

I black out.

Usually when I wake up, someone is dead. Is it me? *Nope.* Not this time. If I'm not dead I go home. I will still be a champion tomorrow.

Bilge wonders if the mission was a success.

So do I.

IRON TIDE

"The Only Way To Know"

Hey Dick! I'm back from cleaning out the hedgehog pits. Whatcha workin' on?
Just finished installing our new *anti-air* emplacement. Agent Stone got us one in case that *mysterious* ***flying-bro*** ever comes back.
You know, the one that attacked us while Wade was poking you in the lab.
Cool! *Can we test it out on some birds?*
HAHAH *of course not!* **That would be super irresponsible!**
Hell ***yeah*** bro.

"She Should Know"

SQUAWK—
DOOMF
Meanwhile, in the RGI Insurance offices...
Oh my God! Did you hear that? It sounded like a flak battery taking pot-shots at birds!
Where the hell is that coming from?
Doesn't matter. That bird was an ass. On more than one occasion I caught him putting the moves on my wife.
What?
He was also a racist.

"Coming Soon"

If you two are quite finished I need you in the other room.
Ooh! You're in trouble!
Whatever bro! It was your idea!
Agents, I have received disturbing news. There has been another Scoria attack, small scale, but significantly more Northern. Close to us.
And there have been sightings, the movements are erratic. But nearby.
We've been preparing for their eventual return and I believe we're as ready as we'll be.
I am warning you now because I am confident we are facing an attack. And in the coming days everyone needs to be on full alert.

"Scheduling Conflict"

Now I am certain that if we see the Scoria at all, it will be *here* and it will be **soon**.
So I need all of you to remain at the ready while I use our humble motion sensor array to watch for any *first warning signs*.
From this terminal I can monitor the movements of anything larger than a dozen mice within a few hundred metres of the base of the building.
I will be watching these monitors ***twenty-four-seven*** until I'm convinced we're under no threat.
What happened to the monitor-watching guy?
He's on vacation.
That doesn't seem like very good timing.
He booked it in advance there was nothing I could do!

"Should Have Called The Guy"

Lady-bro, some of this equipment's been here longer than ***me***. Is it still *good to go*?
El Scantastico
Systems nominal
Scanning designated sectors for medium-large movement signals
Big blinky warning mode active
Entry?
Absolutely. We've even had agent Martin out performing maintenance on it just last week.
Last week
Swipe
Swipe

"The Simplest Answer"

Alright agent Martin, because you are still infected with the Scoria nanites you are a *high-priority target*. You will remain safely ensconced within the building operating the anti-air turret.
Davison is positioned on the roof with the helicopter and Wade is.. *in his lab*. Likely.
MONDAY
Oh ***yeah***, Wade! I almost forgot about him! If he's in his lab so much why doesn't *he* watch the radar thing? *Did you ask him?*
.. didn't want to bother him. He's very likely busy working on a cure for your robot affliction anyway.
It's just because you have a *crush* on him isn't it? ***Admit it***.
Bu
Focus on your task, agent.
It's just like video games, you'll enjoy it.
Yeah except if you miss and hit a pedestrian aircraft *in the game*-
*-You miss and hit a pedestrian aircraft **for real!***
Then don't miss.

"I Only See What I Want To See"

Max bro, since Wade still never got back to us about that cure for your robot-thing I ***really*** hope you don't die in this fight.
Cause then you'd turn into a robot zombie and ***I'd*** have to kill you *again!* And that would **suck**.
TUESDAY
*Thanks man that's **real reassuring!***
Would everybody *please* just ***focus***.
I'm trying but even with these nice-ass binoc's there ain't a *single* babe in ***sight***.
That's *not* what you're supposed to be looking for!

"Settling Down"

WEDNESDAY
Agents. **Status reports.**
Agent Davison report in.
-*Agent Martin?*
Damn it where *is* everybody?
No, **bro** you *can't* trade your sheep for his wood when it's *not your turn!*
It's not **our** bloody fault it takes you *twenty minutes* to ***place a sodding piece of road!***
Excuse **me** but the *Great Wall of Dick* requires careful planning!

"Where The Elite Meet"

THURSDAY
Ahah! Dozens of hostiles detected at the edge of the forest!
This is it.
RAPPEL!
Squirrel-CON 2012!
GO NUTS!
WALNUTS 30 kg

"Enter Sandman"

FRIDAY
Entry?
SIGNATURE: SQUIRREL
ZZZ
WHUMP

"The Twenty-Fifth And Eighth"

SATURDAY
BOOM
ZZ-
GODDAMN SQUIRRELS!
Wait-

"The View From Up Here"

Yo Stone what the hell? **That came out of nowhere!**
What did?
Some beam! Our helicopter's *down* bro!
Didn't you see something on the monitor?
I- Looked away for a moment.
Well look *back* 'cause ***they're here!*** *Dozens* of the bastards. Coming out of the woods.
Did you see what hit us?
No but I have a good guess-
-The mysterious flying bro.
We meet again...
DOOMF

"Where's The Turbo Switch"

Click
Click
Click
Awesome shot Max. But I can *hear you* pressing the button over the headset.
Click Click
Click Click Click
No Birds
Boom
Boom Boom
I applaud your enthusiasm bro but the rate of fire wont change.
SHUT UP I'M HELPING.
Click
click
Click
click

"What An Entrance"

I was in Wade's lab when this thing attacked us last time.. why does it seem so familiar?
Great work agent Martin. Keep up the fire.
-Davison, will you be joining me for the party outside?
Just a sec- Sleeve caught on the- Stairs-
GERONIBROOOOO!
SMASH!

"Battle Hardened Wisdom"

So would it be terribly cliché at this point to insist upon the fact that I totally told you so and then bicker back and forth while we fight?
No need. I believed you bro, but I just have a short attention span.
So you don't want to argue about this?
No. I try to get along with my co-workers.
That's refreshing.
I thought so.
Ka-chK

"Whack Blast Stomp"

WHACK
BLAST
STOMP

"Turned Tables"

No Birds
No Birds
FWOOSH
Va-shoom
Friggin' LAG.
TING!

"The Rain In The Parade Falls Mainly On The Blade"

Slice
Bratta-tatatta -tatatatta
K-chk
BOOM
!

"Ready For Anything"

The situation is dire.
I didn't wish it to have to come to this...
Fiddle
Oh, who am I joshing?
Of course I did.
~Liquor~
KEEP OUT
Fine Whiskey
Thirsty Old Bastard
Bilge come in-where are you? The helicopter is down. The turret is out!
Far ahead of you, dear.
Mr. Andersen, be a lamb and get the hangar door would you?

"Yes Of Course The Building Is Big Enough For Those Things What Are You A Scientist"

Meanwhile, on the **other** side of the Aversion Bureau headquarters...
wrrr
A **top secret plan** is being put into action for the first time.
TALLY-HO!
Bilge- *I hear a* **propellor-**
You let the ***enemy*** *worry about* ***that*** *my dear!*
They don't look worried.
Then *obviously* they weren't there during ***Operation Queen*** back in nineteen forty-four Where I *single-h*
No probably not.
Rmmrrrr

"No Brakes On This Plane"

NEEERom
Crossing the trees and dotting the skies,
Bilge now put fear into cold robot eyes.
This leader of men, he relished a battle.
The sights, the smells, the gunfire crackle-
NNEEEErrom
RATTA TATTA TAtta
Thud
PANG
PANG
Bringing the pain, making lead rain,
RATTA
*Ha-**HAH!** Face my **mustachioed vengeance** you **soulless tin scoundrel!!***
and lending credence, to the claims he's not sane.

"Surprisingly Agile"

I'm **useless** here now, *I'm coming to you!*
***No**, agent, you **must** remain in the building!*
Screw that! I'm not hiding in *here* while you two die out ***there***. *I can help!*
It's not that.
What then?
It appears you may have company.
Was that supposed to sound comforting?
Because it ***didn't***.

"Points For Effort"

Uh-oh.
*That was- **quick**.*
SWING
This one looks ***way*** fancier than the others.
*..**More** fancier?*
Screw it.
BANG
BANG
BANG
PTANG
PING
PANG
?!
WHP-CRAK!
Brzzt
Bzzt
Bvzat

"In Good Favour"

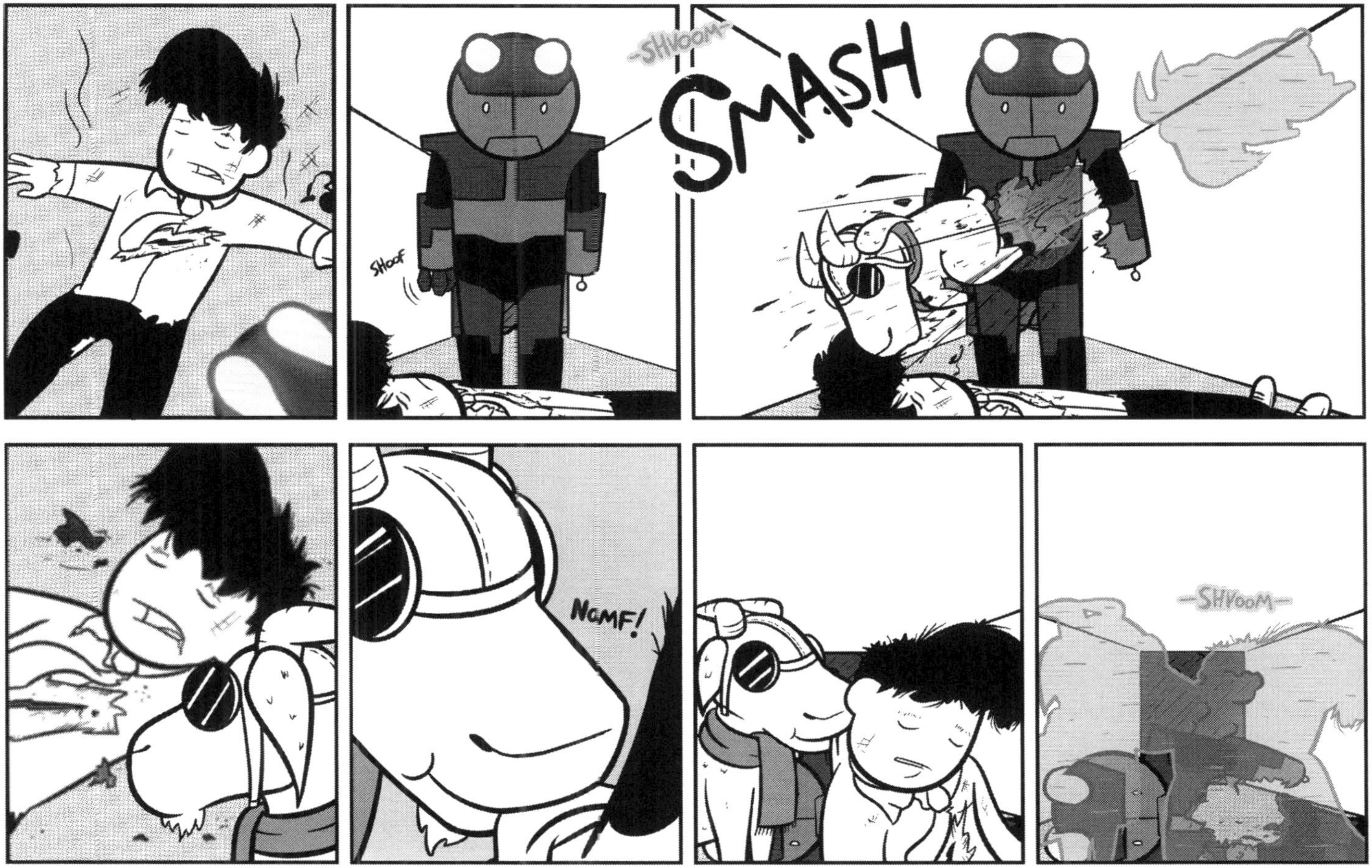
-SHVOOM-
SHOOF
SMASH
NOMF!
-SHVOOM-

"Knowingness"

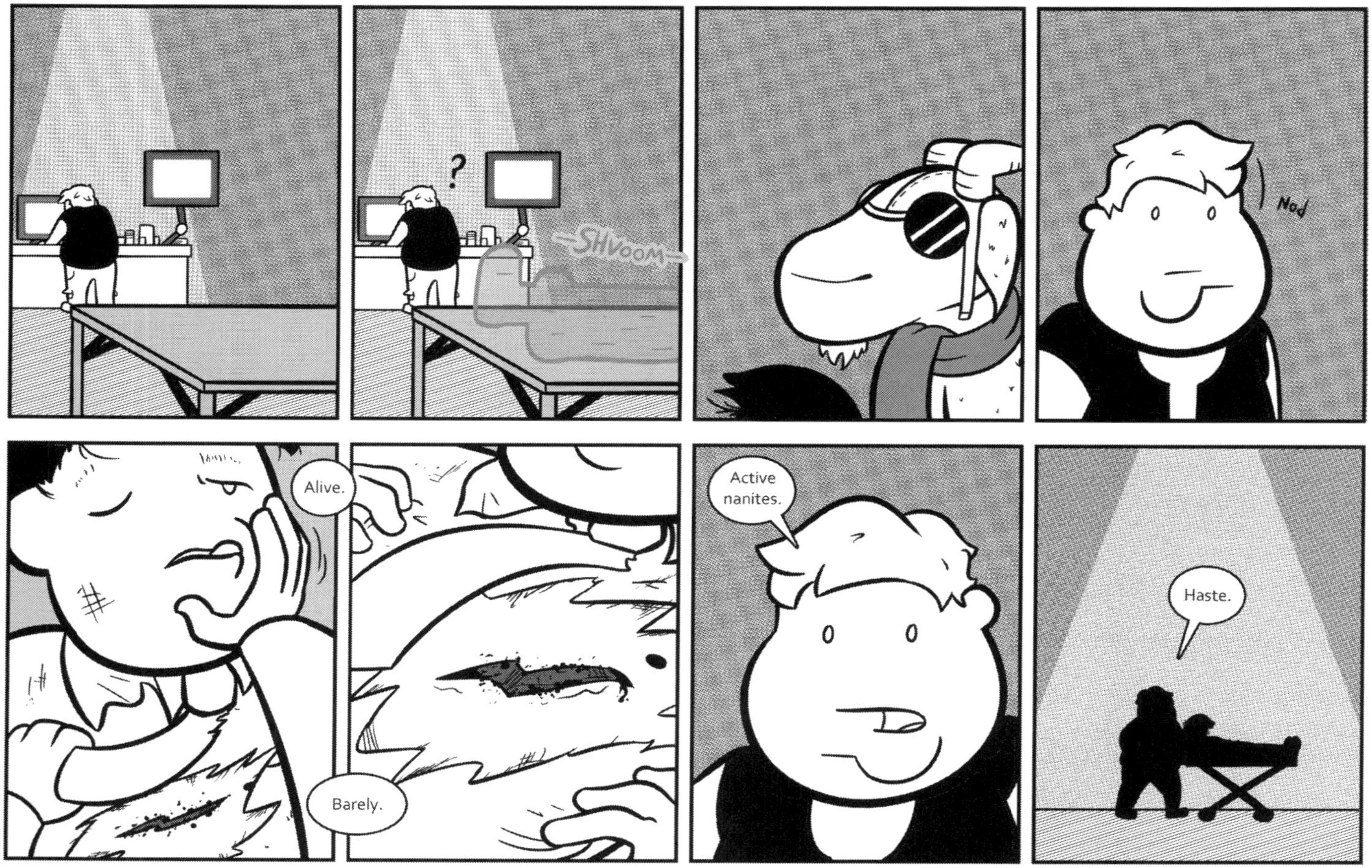
?
SHVOOM
Nod
Alive.
Barely.
Active nanites.
Haste.

"The Nerve Of The Undead"

Meanwhile...
STAB
INTERNET SHIRT
SMACK
INTERNET SHIRT
Did you- Just?
I swear to Robot God I will program you to feel human emotions before I cut your ass to pieces.
Oh.
SWING
PUNCH
That'll work too.
BUMP

"Dog Pile"

STEP
ri...ip
Bratta-tatta
-tattatat
TACKLE
Oof!
Hop
VA-SHOOM

"Break On Through"

Bilge ceftly manoeuvred to the laser-whale flank.
NEEEROOM
RATTA- -TATTA TATTA
TWANG
CLUNK
Its fuel was burning fast once he ruptured the tank.
A very good shot, and angled *just* right.
PING
Whoosh
The crows would scavenge machine-corpse tonight.

"Time Limit"

Treatment administration time frame compromised.
Preferred more tests.
Do not get comfortable with your deity.
Starfish Prime
SP-05

"Red Ryder"

A final assault now laid without speaking,
NEEEERom
RATTA-TATTA
The mechanical horror's engine now creaking.
BWATING!
There are many good reasons to not face down a gun.
NEEEoooooo
Most go without saying- you'll put your eye out, for one.
So with fifty-percent of its recommended sight,
WHOOSH
The once-mighty foe abandoned his fight.
But old Bilge of course, would not leave it at that.
He followed behind and swung his brickbat.
Get **back** here you poor excuse for an *autonomous, thinking, learning* ***combat-robot!***
*Your **mother** was an **N-Gage** and your **father** turned on **StickyKeys!***

"Ro-Bane"

Natalie come in, the whale has turned tail! Hah-ha!
Do you need air-support?
No. Just don't lose the target!
My dear-
-You seem to forget that I am in the sky. I can quite plainly see that your tired and broken forms are out-numbered by even the remnants of the enemy.
Bilge, we're fine.
Apologies, but, sod that.
There will be other days for whaling.
RATTA-
TATTA
Evening, chaps!
PANG
CRACK
BANG
Thwip
Thwip
CLUNK
Thank you.

"Über Nano"

Modified CT-Scanner delivers localized electro-magnetic radiation to afflicted persons.
Current stage of Scoria technology, nano-bots have no such shielding.
Treatment deployment on active nanites unanticipated.
Should not affect outcome.
Glorious time to be alive agent Martin.
I make sure.

"The Silicon Valley"

Phew- That was kinda.. **fun**. *Almost* broke a sweat too. A manly, bro-sweat.
Maybe one drop.
Was that *all* of them?
I think so. The rest, if any, probably retreated with their leader.
Lady bro, why do you think.. that their leader was a ***whale?***
Whales are bad-ass.

"Tickles Down Below"

Director Bilge, meet us inside. We're going to check on agent Martin-
Wha- WOAH!!
SOMETHING'S GOT MY LEG!!
Get it off! GETITOFF!!
Just a moment, Bilge.
Grip
CWWWWWW...
STOMP
Crunch
Oh! Thought it was a spider.

"Fill Me In"

SLAP
-Whatwhere?
Successful resuscitation.
Feeling?
I don't- where?
Deactivated your nanites.
Th- thank you.
Natural body processes will remove nano-waste over time.
You mean I'm cured?!
Yes.
But how did I get here?
Incapacitated- Scoria assassin. Retrieved- Warpgoat.
Really? Man, I owe that thing another sandwich.
Home refrigerator likely already empty.
Well is the fight over? Did we win? Is everyone ok?
Yes.
Debatable.
Single casualty.
Oh GOD who??
You.
Temporarily.

"The Custodian"

I gotta say Stone, you kicked some *real* ass today.
Fine work bro.
Thank you, Davison.
Very well done yourself. They didn't stand a **chance**.
-*Hey* thank **God** it's Saturday today so nobody was in the **RGI offices** to see all of ***that!***
Nudge!
Indeed.
...Awesome.

"Good View Of Your Living Room From Here"

Bro!
Bro!!
That's a *lady-gettin'* scar bro!
BROMP
I know bro!
You look like hell Max, but I'm glad you're alive. *You earned it.*
So *what* exactly happened up here?
Well, first I-
-Excuse me I was talking to Wade.
Agent Incapacitated by taser-whip. Scoria infiltrator. Advanced.
So close to death dormant Scoria nanites activated.
Caught in time. Treatment successful.
Purpose of incapacitation over elimination: retrieval.
Purpose of retrieval: unknown.
-Oh ***Jesus!*** *I just remembered something!* It was this crazy dream I had the night **right** after I first came here!
I think it's somehow.. ***relevant***.
So I'm on this beach building an *awesome* sand castle when ***BOOM!*** Some **guy** knocks it over, and it's a **robot in a trench coat.**
-Suddenly my shovel is ***magic*** and this shadowy figure is shooting beams of **darkness** at me, and I'm all *buff* right?
-I'm slicing up Scoria on the beach and then I *blast* the shadow with this magic shovel I have and I destroy it.
Well- I *think* the shadowy figure was the **whale-robot!** And the sand castle, *it like*, represented my life ***before*** the bureau!
And *uh*... I don't ***really*** know why the Scoria had a trench coat or why I was so **buff** but uh...
Well- at the **end** of the dream, I look at my reflection in the water.. and I'm a robot ***too!***
*I think, like, the shovel represents **you** guys, **empowering** me to fight the darkness...*
Well, like a big metaphor..
Parallels...
I haven't quite figured it all out yet.
That's **stupid** bro.
Yes that doesn't make any sense at all.

"Of All The People"

That was an excellent victory today agents. *Very wonderful job, all of you!*
Our enemy is still *very* mysterious but today we dealt them a **crushing** defeat!
There is *much* to be learned from this I'm sure, as I'm ***convinced*** this is not our last encounter with the Scoria menace.
-But for now.. let us all **rest**. We've earned that much.
...You have your hand up, *Maxfrey?*
Do you have a question?
Director Bilge
Yes sir just a quick question.
...For agent Stone.
I was *wondering*, since Wade is ***always*** in his lab anyway and is *pretty* handy with computers, why didn't we get **him** to watch that radar for us?
When I asked you, *before* all of this, you said he was **busy**.
Wade, *what were you doing?*
Preparing biplane.
Developing nano-virus cure.
Screen watching simple process to automate.
Assumed situation thought-out.
You didn't even ***ask*** him did you?
Hah. Uh.
Why- how about a round of applause for ***team Aversion Bureau?!***
What a team we are!
Gooo team.

"Truth And Reconciliation"

Jesus H Max!
There you are, you've been gone a long time! I was starting to get pretty worried actually.
Man you look like shi-
Hug!
?
MAX's room.
NO GIRLS Allowed.
wait, nevermind.
Hey-
Hi, this is Max, from the club?
...Yes I realize how long it's been.

"Cliff Hanger"

To be continued...

Character Bios

1. Max Martin
Taken under the wing of the Aversion Bureau after a fateful day at the beach, Max is a loyal and gullible person with a heart of gold. He's also a bit of a wuss, but beneath his unimposing demeanor beats the heart of a true hero. And on top of that one beats the heart of desperate and paranoid young man that will take a pass at anything even *resembling* a woman.

2. Director Thomas Bilge
Thomas Bilge is the founder of the Aversion Bureau, a secret organization that endeavors to thwart any and all apocalyptic threats to the world. Bilge's history is shrouded in mystery (whose isn't?) and very little is known about this eccentric older gentleman... That is until you get a drink into his hand. ***Bilge has a problem with booze.***

3. Agent Stone
A calculating and articulate woman who ranks highly within the bureau, a personal favourite of the director. Agent Stone is a natural leader and ass-kicker, she excels in hand to hand combat and having to take care of literally everything for everyone all the time. Stone finds it exhausting dealing with the buffoonery of others and the more eccentric aspects of Bilge's personality, but she holds it all together nonetheless and is a rallying point of reason for the entire team.

4. Dick Davison
Dick Davison is a total bro. He is competitive, pugnacious and a violently sore loser. But having said that, it must also be clear that agent Davison is an incredibly loyal, although headstrong, companion who is un-deniably combat-effective. Deep-down, everybody loves Dick.

5. Wade Andersen
Wade Andersen is a man of few words. He is head of the science, research and technology departments within the bureau and boasts a sizeable lab with which to work. People try to talk to Wade sometimes, though it is questionable whether he recognizes that they exist in the same space at the same time. He has this problem with most people.

Additional Rubes In This Never Ending Farce...

Jim the intern:
Jim is a timid, yet competent worker with a bright future in accounting. Or at least he used to be. Jim is the kind of guy who's always getting swept up in grandiose schemes and ultimately being corrupted by the residual evil in the power-vacuum created when his dark master falls. You know the type. Jim likes football and playing the castanets. His favourite colour is orange.

Jackie the roommate:
Jackie is the girl who shares her apartment with Max on the condition that he pay rent on time and never hit on her. Jackie exists solely so that Max has someone to talk to when the story dictates that he should go home for a bit. There, I said it. She owns a cat but the cat seems to think that it's clothes or something because it's always attached to her in some way.

Reception Lady:
The ever vigilant keeper-of-appointments and confirmer-of-identification. Reception Lady keeps watch at the reception desk by the entrance to the building that houses both RGI and the Aversion Bureau, though she is none the wiser to the latter. Everyone seems to think she's pretty good looking but we've never seen her face so who knows.

Agent Whiskers:
Agent Whiskers is a semi-psychotic investigator type who runs long-term undercover investigations away from the bureau and prefers to work alone as his methods for interrogation and apprehension often fall into a grey area with the Geneva Convention. I've mentioned before that there are "barely a dozen agents" working for the bureau and as the main cast only consists of five, that leaves me some space to have fun. Meow.

Warpgoat:
Warpgoat is an inter-dimensional being of immense power, able to move through time and space on a singular goaty whim. It visits and leaves the Bureau of its own free will and nobody knows quite why it likes the place so much. Yet even with the weight of such abilities it retains the sensibilities of snappy dressing, sporting a stylish orange scarf, goggles and flight cap. Warpgoat does, like all goats do, attempt to chew on everything. Coupled with the powers of manipulating time space, it can be a real son of a bitch when Warpgoat steals your lunch right out of your hands. A time-honoured tradition of the bureau for new initiates is to attempt to catch the Warpgoat, not that it matters though, Warpgoat has thus far eluded them all.

Setting

Founded in secret by the mysterious and eccentric Thomas Bilge, deep in the Northerly regions of North America stands the headquarters of the Aversion Bureau. The Aversion Bureau operates out of the top 31 windowless floors built totally inconspicuously on top of an otherwise run-of-the-mill insurance company. Armed with an unreasonable amount of space, questionable management and effective budgeting, the crack team of dedicated men and women under the Aversion Bureau are ready to combat any threat to the world, whether it be man, machine, or interstellar crustacean WarGod.

The building itself is a 51-storey building sitting (again, totally inconspicuously) just on the outskirts of the very same town we began our adventure in. The 51st floor is the office of director Bilge and the rooftop is home to multiple satellite dishes and antennae as well as a helicopter pad. The interior of the headquarters has facilities such as an armoury, lab, panic room, gym, interrogations office, barracks, server room, firing range, infirmary, winery, ice cream truck and bean-bag chair room, among many others. Bilge admits that he may have gone over-board when first designing the place.

While the Bureau runs with barely a dozen agents and a skeleton crew of lab technicians and security, the first 20 floors of the building play host to a fully-autonomous insurance company. **RGI**, or Really Good Insurance (Seriously, It's great. ™) is the name of the insurance company that operates below the Aversion Bureau. While it is still owned by director Thomas Bilge, it has its own management and runs entirely without his involvement. They sell any and all insurance to any and all clients, and any or all of it is totally great and you should really buy some. Seriously though, they do fairly good business. The Aversion Bureau itself is funded jointly by the profits of this company and by Bilge's own significant personal wealth. All together this comes out to be just enough and with effective budgeting, working in small teams and bringing their lunches from home, they manage to get by.

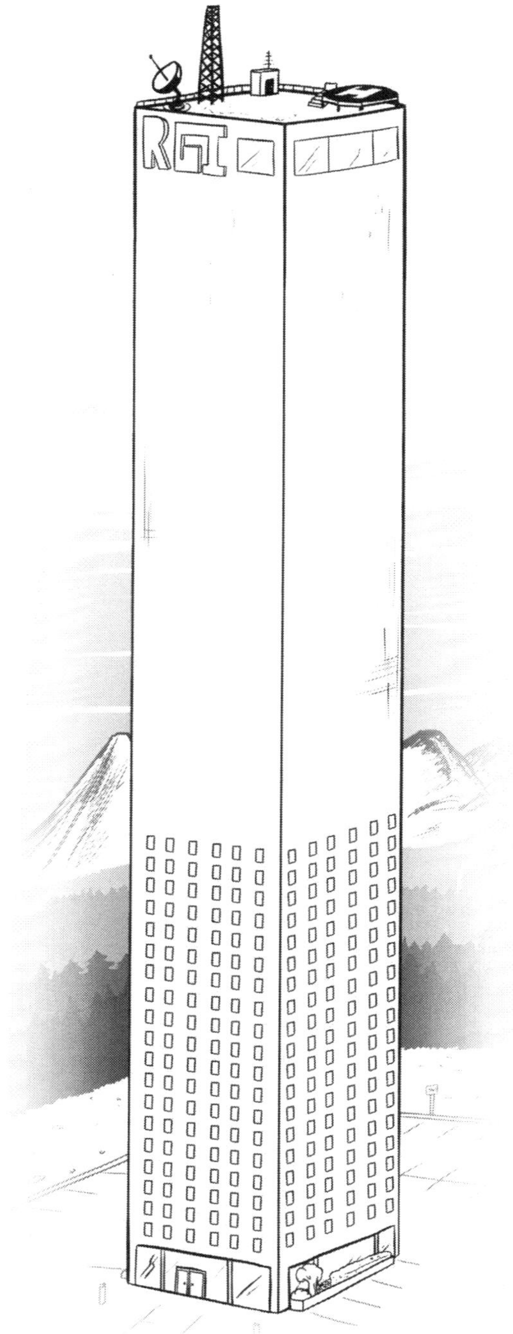

The Scoria

The Scoria are a machine scourge with unknown origins and unknown purposes. In fact, the entire extent of Aversion Bureau stories that involve them have been included in this book! After the end of the first year of *The Aversion Bureau*, the focus has shifted off of them to take a break, with the intention of an eventual return. Hence all of those cliff hangers you just experienced. But they are most certainly the theme of this collection; you knew that before you opened the book.

These things are essentially zombie-robots and that is a concept that is fun from start to finish. The idea being that a payload of nano-robots would reconstruct dead bodies and repurpose them for war, or some other kind of invasion-ey analog. To the mind of whomever currently is behind this mess, there is no more efficient way to create some dead bodies than to deliver the science with a little dollop of explosion. Perhaps the bodies need to be fresh.
Or somebody's just a jerk.

The science is clearly, currently, very crude. There were a few strips where agent Andersen was pondering a reason for this, but I believe we can all agree that it's going to improve, and when that happens.. Well it's a *lot* harder to fight **metal** zombies.

The first insurgence of Scoria appears to have been led by a highly advanced flying whale. More specifically: a rocket whale. He didn't have wings. Does that have significance? **Maybe.**

To whatever capacity that sea-beast actually leads the robot army we cannot yet know, but it's clearly something to worry about. *Whales are badass.*

**Scientists (good guy scientists) do not currently know how Scoria communicate, whether they eat or drink nor the reason behind their constant 45% tipping. Maybe they're actually pretty cool (?)*

Extra Art

I had a dig through my first Aversion Bureau sketchbook and all the relevant folders on the ghostbox (computer) to come up with something awesome for this section. Have a look around and I'll try to note down some "fun facts" wherever they appear. Hell, some of them may be *legitimately* fun!

Immediately following that are some excellent pieces of fan-art by friends of mine more than talented enough to make their ***own*** webcomics.

*I cannot, for the life of me, remember when I drew this picture of Bilge, but it's so awesome I think it will eventually need its own story just so we can get some more of **that.***

This is a t-shirt design that I've printed and sold at conventions! It's an octopus/grenade based off of the Octopus Grenade joke in one of my favourite Aversion Bureau comics, strip #53.

This is what a typical page of my workbook looks like. I scribble the comics and text down and then use it as reference as I go straight to digital. I find scanning to be too time-consuming to bother with.

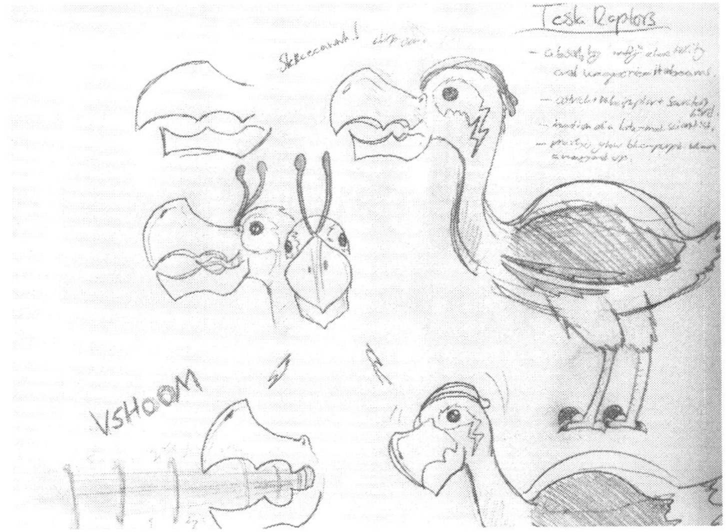

One of my favourite creatures in the comic series are these birds. Even though I never named them in the strip, I decided that they were "Tesla Raptors" because of the electricity thing. I really, **really** want to use them again.

This picture is a good deal more significant than the others! It is something I sketched out, very roughly, while I was still making up The Aversion Bureau. After the characters but before the story. This one particular picture inspired the entire "A Day At The Beach" storyline and thereafter the majority of this book collection's over-arching robot theme.

Please note how ridiculously small and un-manly Dick Davisons chin is here. Even all the hair is weirdly short.

This is the most shockingly **old-looking** art I've included in the book. It is a crudely stitched-together image of all the original sketches for each Aversion Bureau character. (Agent Whiskers came along much later.) Each of these was from a separate page of an old sketchbook complete with character notes that range from wildly inaccurate to outright spoilers. When I began The Aversion Bureau, I hadn't drawn in a very long time. It's amazing how fast you can re-learn something like that when you update your comic five to six times per week.

These two images have a story behind them: I've never been one for planning or brainstorming very much. Too long spent over-thinking a story idea and I very quickly become bored with it. My personal best results come from taking an idea and running with it. The Aversion Bureau is an example of this. All I knew was that I wanted to get back into webcomics, I had a rough idea for a setting and premise and I knew what kind of release schedule I wanted to use.

On one of my days off I sat down and I created every single character sheet, the name, the logo and the first few story ideas in **one afternoon.** I felt like I would figure the rest out on the go, so I took off with it and never ever stopped. It worked out alright!

#1

Look at these

#50

it's you.

#101

#149

#200

click
click

#250

#275

The evolution of Max Martin! *Throughout the stories that this book encompasses, his hair becomes more and more ridiculous, but it's very much a part of him once the art style gets established. I really enjoy his silhouette. Surely the art is getting better as time goes on, but as we finish the book we've entered into a phase I begrudgingly remember as "The tiny-eye times". I learned to fix that later on.*

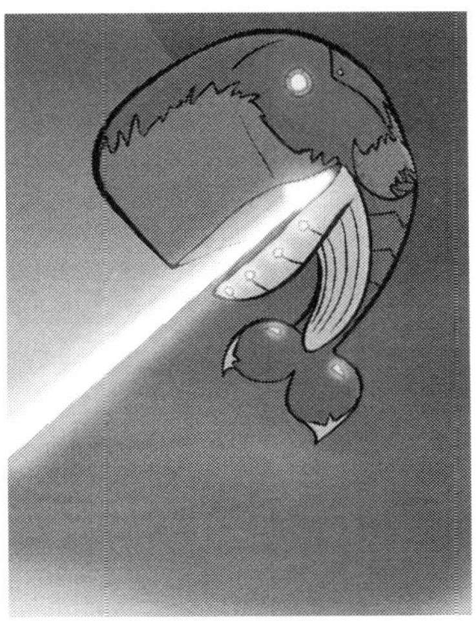

(Exploding Wumpus)
2009

(The Aversion Bureau)
2012

You may be confused as to why there are two whales here! Let me explain:

To those of you who might have read my other webcomic "Exploding Wumpus", the Scoria general/rocket-whale will appear very familiar! Near the end of that comic, this character was introduced under completely unrelated pretenses, but I liked the idea so much that when the strip ended before he could do anything interesting it was almost ***mandatory*** *to revive him and let him do something awesome here.*

"Photoshop Ate This File Before I Could Finish"
— Aria Bell

Fun fact: *The reason for two images from the same artist is right there in the title. I personally insisted on keeping them both because this piece is still TOTALLY awesome.*

"Onward!"
— Aria Bell

Fun fact: *This image is actually a reference to a story from the SECOND year of The Aversion Bureau. So, you know, SPOILERS.*

"The (Sobriety) Aversion Bureau"
— Junkyard Sam

"The Aversion Trio"
— Casey Poznikoff

Fun fact: *In colour, this piece has everyone's correct eye colours and everything! It's very detailed. It has officially entered into my brain as what these characters would actually look like.*

"Sensual Bishounen Max"

— Chris

I STILL
HAVEN'T
READ IT.

"Aversion Bureau Pumpkin"

— Connor Krushel

Fun fact: *He really hasn't.*

"The Aversion Bureau And Warpgoat"
— Ashley W

Fun fact: *You may remember that tiny man in the corner as the custodian from strip #273 that totally saw EVERYTHING.*

"Aversion"
— Mike Ackman

Fun fact: *Max is reminiscent of Matthew Perry in this image. The creator of The Aversion Bureau is a big fan of Matthew Perry.*

"Aversion Bureau Cast Painting"
— Annette Ringuette

Max Martin's Ladies Man Word Search

```
P Q V A S S U N G L A S S E S I P
E P P L D A K L C L U D P L S S L
P R S L P X M V S A E P X E P L E
F A P H A L P E P I B R O B P P A
E E A O M E P R D N O U Y A P D S
P L C U I A P E A L L N I G H T E
I E E S S N K A C P U N C H E F R
P E P E G U I T L P L T P G L I J
A G A S U T S B U W P E N U H H L
N U N U I S S U B K B P A P S Z I
E N T A D J A T P O R P P S P Z V
U P S L E A N S P E I R E X U Y F
D A C U D M D J D O O P S P M R R
P V H T P A T P T E N O M U P Q E
I P Y E P R E J E C T I O N A P X
P S P A R K L E T E T S B E F V H
P E E D E C L U R P E I F A R T E
B W R P A I P E P Y E L L O W P S
P O B I V T P B U R E A U P C A T
M M O T E R K P L O T I O N P K M
X B L P P U J E C U L A T E P Z A
E T E P M S R E Y V P M I S E R Y
```

WORD BANK

- *SUNGLASSES*
- ***SUAVE***
- *DACLUB*
- ***SPACEPANTS***
- *PLEASURE*
- ***ALLNIGHT***
- *KISSANDTELL*
- ***MISGUIDED***
- *HYPERBOLE*
- ***REJECTION***
- *MISERY*
- ***LOTION***

Bilge's Booze Maze

Lead director Bilge to the booze before agent Stone kills his buzz!

START
A trap door you don't remember building!
START OVER
Caught by agent Stone!
START OVER
The hedgehog pits! Adorable, but distracting.
START OVER
FINISH
OLD
BASTARD

Dick Davison's Connect The Dots Bro

STEPS

Step 1:
Connect the dots.
Start at "1"

Step 2:
Keep connecting the dots bro.

Step 3:
You done? Great.

Step 4:
Now add some babes.

Step 5:
Muscle definition.
(to taste)

Step 6:
Good job bro!
All done, grab a beer.

Step 69:
Heh.

Agent Whisker's Spot The Difference

(FOR SERIOUS DETECTIVES ONLY!)

ANSWER KEY:

(1) Agent Davison should not have large breasts. (2) Agent Stone forgot her contacts that morning.
(3) Bilge's sweater could be offensive to dinosaurs. (4) Max Martin has agent Whisker's face. How did that happen?
(5) Wade Andersen has eyebrows. (6) God damn, *Bilge looks so weird.*

(BONUS SUPER DETECTIVE FIND) Everybody only has four fingers. *Wait damn.*

AbOUTroduction (the author)

(Just to be clear, this section is a combination of an "about the author" and an "outroduction" It's confusing, but I just adore that train wreck of wordplay.)

My name is Sebastien Ringuette. I am a British/French-Canadian crossbreed that successfully reached maturity in the harsh (although friendly) climate of Western Canada. My mission has always been to create comics in some form or another, I love to write things that aren't books and I love to draw things that aren't good enough to stand up without a joke attached.

This is not my first attempt at webcomics, from 2007 – 2010 I wrote/drew a webcomic called *Exploding Wumpus* over at a website of a similar name. *The Aversion Bureau* rose from the ashes of that enterprise like a black and white phoenix that tells jokes five times a week.

Which is to say, a *particularly awesome* phoenix.

I draw a lot of my artistic inspiration in recent years from the art of Dan Paladin, Mike Krahulik, Kris Straub and Anthony Clark. There are even more to list, but that could take a very long time and hyperlinks don't work on paper no matter **how** hard you press them.

The book is mostly over now, but the universe of *The Aversion Bureau* is forever ongoing! It's always easy to get more, and there's a lot more to get. Just head over to the website, it's easy to find out what I'm up to even if it's not related to this particular comic strip.

But I'll always be doing ***something.***

aversionbureau.com

Thanks for reading!

THE END

OR IS IT?

Yes.

30810510R00118

Made in the USA
Charleston, SC
28 June 2014